SEEKING SHELTER:
Cambodians in Thailand

A Report on Human Rights

Lawyers Committee for Human Rights
330 Seventh Avenue
New York, NY 10001
(212)629-6170

The Lawyers Committee for Human Rights

Since 1978 the Lawyers Committee has served as a public interest law center. The Lawyers Committee works to promote international human rights law and legal procedures in the United States and abroad. The chairman of the Lawyers Committee is Marvin E. Frankel; Michael Posner is its Executive Director.

Bound copies of this report are available from:

Lawyers Committee for Human Rights
330 Seventh Avenue
New York, NY 10001

TABLE OF CONTENTS

PREFACE

This report describes the latest of the seemingly unending threats to the safety and well-being of the Cambodian people. Its subject is the security of more than a quarter of a million displaced Cambodians[1] living in Thailand.

The genesis of this report is the preparation of the 1985 report of the Lawyers Committee for Human Rights summarizing the status of human rights in Cambodia six years after the Vietnamese invasion of the country and the consequent fall from power of Pol Pot and the Khmer Rouge, whose barbarous policies caused the deaths of over a million of the seven million Cambodian people.[2] That report concluded that, judged against well-established standards of human rights — against, in fact, almost any standard of human rights significantly more demanding than that adhered to by the murderous Khmer Rouge — the Vietnamese-installed, supported and perpetuated regime of Heng Samrin falls far short of meeting minimal human rights standards. In the course of preparing that report, representatives of the Lawyers Committee heard reports of mistreatment of Cambodians who had fled into Thailand.

---

1. In recent decades, the nation we refer to as "Cambodia" has been known by several names. From 1953, when Prince Norodom Sihanouk declared the nation's independence from France, until 1970, the country was officially known (in English) as the Kingdom of Cambodia. From 1970, when General Lon Nol deposed the Sihanouk regime in a military coup, until 1975, the country's official name was the Khmer Republic, referring to the nation's dominant ethnic group. In early 1976, when Khmer Rouge forces came to power, their leaders changed the country's name to Democratic Kampuchea (DK). And when the Vietnamese army overran the DK regime in January 1979, it installed a new regime called the People's Republic of Kampuchea, which remains in power with the support of Vietnamese forces. In 1982, three guerrilla forces opposing that regime joined in a loose coalition called the Coalition Government of Democratic Kampuchea, which is the government of the state that holds the nation's seat at the United Nations. In referring to the country as "Cambodia," the Lawyers Committee does not intend to signify any political position regarding these contending forces' respective claims to legitimacy. We use the term "Cambodia" because it is the term by which most of our audience knows the country.

2. Lawyers Committee for Human Rights, *Kampuchea: After the Worst* (August 1985).

1

This report is the result of the effort of the Lawyers Committee to examine those charges.

The principal author of this report was Stephen Golub, a consultant to the Lawyers Committee. Diane Orentlicher, Director of the Committee's International Human Rights Program, was a contributing author and also edited the report, together with Floyd Abrams, a member of the Board of Directors of the Lawyers Committee.

An earlier draft of this report was submitted to the Thai government in early December 1986, and formed the basis of discussions with government officials and representatives of international relief organizations during a visit to Thailand by Mr. Abrams and Ms. Orentlicher in January 1987. The draft that was presented to the government was based in part on a mission of inquiry to Thailand, as well as subsequent research undertaken by Mr. Golub. From October 19 through November 4, 1985, Mr. Golub visited camps holding approximately 75 percent of the Cambodian population residing in Thailand. These included "Site Two," a cluster of Cambodian settlements affiliated with the Khmer People's National Liberation Front (KPNLF), a non-communist group opposing the Vietnamese occupation of Cambodia; "Site Eight," a settlement affiliated with the guerrilla forces of Democratic Kampuchea (DK), commonly known as the Khmer Rouge, which also oppose the Vietnamese presence in Cambodia; and Khao I Dang, a holding center administered by Thailand in cooperation with the United Nations High Commissioner for Refugees (UNHCR), from which many thousands of Cambodians have been resettled in third countries.[3]

While in Thailand, Mr. Golub conducted in-depth interviews with some 90 displaced persons. Dozens of other displaced Cambodians provided information that supplemented the more formal

---

3. Mr. Golub did not visit "Site B," which is affiliated with a third anti-Vietnamese guerrilla force loyal to Prince Norodom Sihanouk, known by the French acronym FUNCINPEC, in part because of time constraints and, more importantly, because problems there reportedly have been significantly less severe than at the other large camps.

interviews. Except for a few cases where family members were present, the interviews were conducted in private; all were conducted outside the presence of Thai, Cambodian or other authorities responsible for administering or otherwise supervising the camps in which displaced Cambodians reside.

While in Thailand, Mr. Golub met with Major General Surin Vorathas and Colonel Pittya Silakorn, respectively the Director and Chief of Operations of Thailand's Command Center for the Relief of Kampucheans. Before, during and after his visit to Thailand, Mr. Golub also conducted over 120 interviews with other persons knowledgeable about the situation that is the subject of this report, including officials of international and private organizations operating in the camps; U.S. State Department representatives (in Washington, D.C.); journalists; scholars; relief workers; and officials of the KPNLF and FUNCINPEC.

Most of the accounts of attacks on Cambodians included in this report are based on interviews with the victims and eyewitnesses, corroborated by such documentation as relevant medical records. Where it was not possible for the Lawyers Committee to interview the victims or eyewitnesses of a reported attack, the incident has not been cited unless at least two — and typically more — reliable sources investigated the matter independently.

Fearing retaliation, most of the victims interviewed for this report spoke to the Lawyers Committee on the condition that they not be identified in the report. We have identified such sources by pseudonyms, denoted by ''(P).'' Other details that might identify such persons, including precise dates and locations of certain incidents, and in some cases the nationality of the victims, have also been excluded.   *   *   *   *

From January 5 through 9, 1987, Floyd Abrams and Diane Orentlicher, co-authors of the Committee's previous report on human rights conditions inside Cambodia, met with various officials of the Thai government, the KPNLF, and international relief agencies to discuss the principal findings of this report. Before visiting Thailand, they met with Thailand's Ambassador to Washington, Arsa Sarasin, who provided invaluable assistance in the preparation of their trip to Thailand. In Bangkok, Mr. Abrams and Ms. Orentlicher met with Thailand's Foreign Minister, Siddhi Savetsila;

3

the Permanent Secretary to the Foreign Minister, Kasem Kasemsri, and other officials of the Foreign Ministry; the Chief of Staff of the Royal Thai Army, General Wanchai Ruangtrakul and two of his deputies; the Deputy Secretary General of Thailand's National Security Council, Khachadpai Burusapatana; and the outgoing commander of Task Force 80, Col. Pao Pasant. All of the Thai officials whom we met were generous with their time, and their candor and concern about the problems documented in this report contributed to productive discussions. We wish to record our appreciation, as well, for their extraordinary graciousness in accommodating our many requests to interview a wide range of individuals.

Mr. Abrams and Ms. Orentlicher also met with officials of the KPNLF, whose troops have been responsible for many of the abuses chronicled in this report. These meetings included interviews with Son Sann, the President of the KPNLF; General Sak Sutsakhan, the Commander-in-Chief of the KPNLF army; several military commanders, including one (Liv Ne) whose troops have been implicated in some of the most serious abuses described in this report; and several members of a newly-appointed committee to investigate allegations of abuses by KPNLF soldiers.

The two delegates also met with several representatives of the United States Embassy in Thailand, including Ambassador William Brown. Among the officials responsible for refugee matters at the Embassy whom the Committee representatives met, Lacy Wright deserves special appreciation for his assistance and valuable insights.

Finally, Mr. Abrams and Ms. Orentlicher met with representatives of the international relief organizations that provide assistance to Cambodians in Thailand, including Tatsuro Kunugi, the Special Representative of the United Nations Secretary General for Coordination of Kampuchean Humanitarian Assistance Programmes, and his Deputy, Jamshid Anvar; Y.Y. Kim, the Director of the United Nations Border Relief Operation; Gerald Walzer, the Representative to Thailand of the United Nations High Commissioner for Refugees; and Urs Boegli, Head of the Thailand Delegation of the International Committee of the Red Cross.

The draft report that had served as the basis for those discussions was revised to reflect recent developments of which Mr. Abrams and Ms. Orentlicher learned during their visit to Thailand.

Many of those revisions reflect measures taken by Thai and KPNLF authorities in recent weeks to address abuses described in the draft report that was sent to the Thai government in early December.

*   *   *   *

We wish to express our appreciation for the assistance of several people and organizations in providing information and insights, and in reviewing earlier drafts of this report. Among those whom we can publicly acknowledge are Susan Goodwillie, David Hawk, Claire Osborne, Raul Pangalangan, Al Santoli, Roger Winter and Amnesty International.

The Lawyers Committee gratefully acknowledges the support of the Human Rights Program of Harvard Law School for the investigation undertaken on the Thai-Cambodian border.

I. INTRODUCTION

Two years have passed since Vietnamese troops launched a devastating military offensive against Cambodians opposing Vietnam's occupation of their country. A quarter of a million Cambodians fled into Thailand and, once again, were briefly seen on front pages throughout the world. The haunting images of tired and frightened faces fleeing artillery fire evoked earlier, but hardly distant, images of a people who had been ravaged by virtually every conceivable variation on human tragedy. Forced entanglement in the Indochina war, massive aerial bombardment, genocidal rule by Pol Pot's Khmer Rouge, famine, and foreign occupation had successively scourged their nation in the short span of one and a half decades.

The Cambodians who took flight two years ago no longer make headlines, but their trials have hardly ended. Though Thailand has given them temporary haven until they can safely return to their own country,[4] the displaced Cambodians[5] face an uncertain future, and a present fraught with perils.

---

4. Thailand currently hosts some 270,000 Cambodians in United Nations-assisted camps. An estimated 10,000 more civilian Cambodians live in military logistics bases on Thai soil, beyond the protective reach of international assistance or observation.

5. We refer to the Cambodians in Thailand as "displaced persons" rather than "refugees" because the Thai government has not granted them legal status as refugees. Additionally, the protection mandate of the United Nations High Commissioner for Refugees (UNHCR) in Thailand embraces only ten percent of the Cambodian population there. (Cambodians in the UNHCR-assisted Khao I Dang holding center, its Annex and the Phanat Nikhom Transit Center constitute this protected group.) While most Cambodians in Thailand do not enjoy legal refugee status there, the term is commonly applied to them, and is even occasionally used by Thai officials.

Many may, in fact, meet the definition of "refugee" set forth in the 1951 Convention Relating to the Status of Refugees (189 U.N.T.S 137) and its 1967 Protocol (267 U.N.T.S. 606, 137), neither of which has been ratified by Thailand. Those treaties define a refugee as any person who, "owing to well-founded fear of being persecuted for reasons of race, religion, nationality, membership of a particular social group or political opinion, is outside the country of his nationality and is unable or, owing to such fear, is unwilling to avail himself of the protection of that country. . . ."

7

Thousands of troops of the Vietnamese and Cambodian armies loom a short distance away from the sites astride the Thai-Cambodian border in which the bulk of the displaced Cambodians are settled. The largest concentration, Site Two, lies just one mile from the border. A plain presenting no natural obstacle to attack separates its 141,000 residents[6] from the troops that drove them into Thailand two years ago. The perilous nature of this threat was underscored by a recent shelling of Site Two North by Vietnamese forces. On January 26, 1987, several shells landed directly in the site's Dong Ruk settlement, seriously wounding at least eight of the camp's residents.

Bands of armed Cambodian robbers, sometimes 20 or 30 strong, pose a separate threat to the Cambodians on the border, as well as those in Khao I Dang — a holding center farther away from the border which was officially closed on December 31, 1986, but whose residents have not yet been transferred to other sites. Toting automatic rifles and rocket-propelled grenade guns, the so-called "bandits" terrorized several camps, particularly Khao I Dang and Site Two, in 1985. Enhanced security measures improved the situation at Khao I Dang in April of 1985, and at Site Two South in October 1985. But several violent bandit raids at the Khao I Dang Annex in February and March of 1986, and at Site Two beginning in September 1986, underlined the need for renewed efforts to address the problem of banditry.

A further threat has come, ironically, from the very paramilitary units that the Thai government has assigned to guard and protect the Cambodians — the rangers of Task Force 80. While some rangers have risked and lost their lives to protect the displaced Cambodians from Cambodian bandits, there has also been an alarming incidence of ranger abuse. Rangers have robbed, beaten and raped the residents of some camps, with apparent impunity. As recently as

---

6. Figures pertaining to camp populations used in this report are derived from United Nations Border Relief Operation, *Situation Report as at August 15, 1986* at 8. The relevant population numbers have varied somewhat since that report's publication, but are roughly similar.

November 1986, an illegal resident of Khao I Dang was badly beaten by several rangers and then fatally shot in the back of the head at close range. The rangers' conduct has generated an atmosphere of fear even among those who have not personally been victimized.

There has been little indication that such abuses have resulted in appropriate discipline by the Task Force 80 officers who supervise the rangers. And in one highly publicized incident on March 21-22, 1986, three Task Force 80 officers themselves inflicted severe torture on three Cambodians who had been arrested on suspicion of having participated in a violent raid in Khao I Dang. Their torture included having a hot iron and burning firewood applied to various parts of their bodies; having their hair set on fire; having boiling, salted water poured over their open wounds; and being whipped with an electric cable. Despite incontrovertible evidence that the three were tortured, the Thai government quickly absolved Task Force 80 of any wrongdoing.

A fourth peril has threatened persons seeking to enter Thailand near the Rithisen, Chamkar Ko, and Nong Chan military bases. These bases straddle the Thai-Cambodian border and are controlled by the Khmer People's National Liberation Front (KPNLF), one of three guerrilla forces united in a loose coalition that opposes the Vietnamese occupation of their country. The three bases are part of "the hidden border," a string of logistics/military guerrilla camps where 10,000 or more displaced Cambodian civilians live, but to which international relief organizations have no access. For more than a year, KPNLF troops operating in or near Rithisen, Chamkar Ko, and Nong Chan have repeatedly raped, robbed and detained both Vietnamese fleeing to Thailand via Cambodia and Cambodians seeking to enter Thailand. Those detained were frequently held until relatives abroad secured their release through the payment of "ransoms." There also are indications that Khmer Rouge troops have committed rapes and robberies in the general area.

As 1986 drew to a close, several measures were taken to address these abuses. In late October, the International Committee of the Red Cross and the United Nations Border Relief Operation moved over a thousand civilians out of the camps where the abuses had proliferated and into Site Two. Then, in late November, the Chief of Staff of the Royal Thai Army met with KPNLF military leaders and made it clear that the abuses must end. The KPNLF now asserts that it has transferred most of the troops responsible for the abuses — and the two commanders of the most abusive troops — away from the border zone, leaving only enough soldiers at the border camps to guard the entry points into Thailand. While it is too early to measure the effect of these actions, they signal a welcome indication that the responsible authorities recognize the gravity of the problem, and accept responsibility for bringing the abuses to an end.

Abuses of a different order continue to affect some 59,000 Cambodians living in camps in Thailand that are controlled by the Khmer Rouge. Remnants of a regime responsible for wiping out at least one million of Cambodia's total population of seven million just a decade ago, today the Khmer Rouge guerrillas exert rigid control over the lives of those camp residents. Pervasive intimidation has at times been reinforced by removal of some of the civilians to places where they must undergo "re-education," and of others to the Cambodian interior, where they reportedly are pressed into the hazardous duty of transporting military supplies.

Most vulnerable to such practices are civilians who express a desire to live in the non-communist camps affiliated with the KPNLF or with Prince Sihanouk's National United Front for an Independent, Neutral, Peaceful and Cooperative Cambodia (known by its French acronym, "FUNCINPEC"). They may well represent the tip of the iceberg: it is commonly estimated that at least one-third of the 30,000 residents of Site Eight — the largest Khmer Rouge camp on the border — would move to KPNLF or FUNCINPEC camps if given the opportunity. While the mobility of those living in camps loyal to the two non-communist guerrilla factions also is limited, the restraint imposed in Khmer Rouge camps poses unique humanitarian concerns in view of that group's exceptionally appalling human rights record.

As the Cambodians' stay in Thailand has lengthened, the resulting strains on that country have threatened to exacerbate the security problems. The burden of providing first asylum to those fleeing the political upheavals in Indochina has fallen most heavily on Thailand. As of July 1986, it hosted 128,000 people who had fled

Vietnam, Cambodia and Laos — not including the quarter million Cambodians and Vietnamese "land people"[7] on its border with Cambodia — far exceeding the combined total in other countries of first asylum.[8]

As resettlement of Indochinese refugees by other nations has fallen off, Thailand has understandably evinced concern about the implications of the increasingly static nature of the displaced Cambodians. Such concerns undoubtedly lie behind its decision to close Khao I Dang on December 31, 1986. Although scores of thousands of Cambodians have been accepted from Khao I Dang for third-country resettlement since it opened in 1979, the residual population has been rejected for such resettlement,[9] and — in Thailand's view — the holding center nonetheless has continued to serve as a magnet for Cambodians hoping to emigrate.

Though Thailand has not yet implemented its decision to close Khao I Dang, it has announced that it plans to move the camp's residents from their more secure site away from the conflictive border region to the existing camps along the border, with all of their attendant risks. In doing so, it has resisted entreaties by numerous relief organizations.

Ultimately, of course, the plight of the Cambodians in Thailand cannot be resolved until a solution to the political conflict that lies behind their presence on the border is achieved. But their situation surely can and must be improved. As the current civil war in Cambodia stretches into its eighth year, and a political solution remains elusive, the world community cannot fail to do all that is possible to protect the shattered victims of Cambodia's turmoils.

---

7. This refers to Vietnamese who fled to Thailand overland, via Cambodia.

8. Hong Kong, Malaysia, Indonesia, the Philippines, Japan, Macau, Korea, Singapore and Taiwan together account for only 27,679 refugees. See United States Department of State, *Report of the Indochinese Refugee Panel* (April 1986) at 12.

9. As noted in Chapter VII, the process by which the Khao I Dang population has been rejected for resettlement in the United States has been widely criticized.

*   *   *   *

When we began the investigation that led to this report, there was little indication that the plight of the Cambodians in Thailand would elicit the concern it merited from responsible policymakers. The abuses we describe seemed a virtually forbidden topic in Thailand. Even personnel with humanitarian organizations discussed the abuses in hushed tones, fearing their possible expulsion from Thailand if they raised the issues before appropriate authorities. The local press was all but silent on the subject. And the U.S. Embassy in Bangkok did little to break the silence, appearing all but indifferent to the abuses.

In recent weeks, there appears to have been a turnabout in the prevailing attitudes toward these issues. When two representatives of the Lawyers Committee visited Thailand in January 1987 to discuss an earlier draft of this report with responsible officials, representatives of the Thai government went to great lengths to make themselves available to discuss our concerns. Significantly, they did not challenge the accuracy of any of the abuses described in this report. Instead, our discussions focused on efforts to address the problems. Several such efforts, described in this report, had been undertaken in the weeks preceding our arrival; other possible reforms were still under consideration at the time of our visit.

A similar attitude prevailed among the KPNLF officials with whom we met. The abuses committed by the Front's troops were acknowledged, and a number of steps newly undertaken to address the abuses were described to us.

For its part, the U.S. Embassy in Bangkok shifted into active gear after a long period of seeming acquiescence in the abuses against the displaced Cambodians. In November 1986, two officials of the Reagan Administration raised their concerns about KPNLF rapes and detentions-for-ransom at border entry points with the Thai government.

November also brought a marked change in the U.S. Embassy's stance on the closing of Khao I Dang. Until then, it had done little to address the serious security issues raised by Thailand's plan — first announced in June 1986 — to close the camp by the end of December 1986. This changed when the Director of the State Department's Refugee Bureau visited Thailand in November. Since then, the U.S. Embassy has urged the Thai government to continue to respect the Khao I Dang residents' special status as refugees subject to the protection of the United Nations High Commissioner for Refugees (UNHCR) even after they were transferred to another site.[10]

All of these developments signify the possibility of a significant change. But it would be premature to regard the abuses which they address as a concern of the past. The multiple security problems chronicled in this report will continue to stalk the Cambodians in Thailand unless procedures are set in place to monitor and respond to those abuses on an ongoing basis.

Ironically, the closing of Khao I Dang presents an opportune moment to establish such a mechanism. Thailand is now determining what role the UNHCR will play once the residents of Khao I Dang, who now fall within the UNHCR's protection mandate, are transferred to another site. We believe it vital that those Cambodians continue to enjoy the protection of the UNHCR once they are removed from Khao I Dang. We also believe that the security of the quarter of a million Cambodians who now live on the Thai-Cambodian border would be greatly enhanced if UNHCR's mandate were extended to embrace them as well. This measure would go a long way toward translating Thailand's new resolve to address the security problems of the displaced Cambodians into an effective program of protection.

While it is far too soon to assess the efficacy of other initiatives recently taken to address the abuses suffered by the Cambodians in Thailand, two conclusions are certain. First, the recent recognition by responsible authorities that the abuses must be addressed is itself a welcome and significant step forward. Second, the abuses themselves are a long-term problem, and cannot be eradicated unless they become the object of concerted and sustained attention.

New York
February 1987

---

10. The United States also began to press for Thailand to keep Khao I Dang open until the U.S. Embassy's staff could interview all of the camp's residents who are eligible to be considered for resettlement in the United States, and urged that its staff be allowed to continue to interview residents for resettlement even after they were moved from Khao I Dang.

CONCLUSIONS AND RECOMMENDATIONS

Security Threats Posed By Proximity to the Border

1. The location of the camps for displaced Cambodians in Thailand just a few miles from the Thai-Cambodian border dangerously exposes them to attack by Vietnamese troops, as well as casualties caused by stray shells or the crossfire of battle. The largest civilian encampment — Site Two — is especially vulnerable to attack, situated just over one mile from the Thai-Cambodian border. Such attacks and shelling have claimed numerous casualties in recent years. As recently as January 26, 1987, several shells landed inside Site Two. Initial reports indicated that eight or nine residents of Site Two North were seriously wounded. In a single incident in January 1985 the Vietnamese army reportedly massacred at least 150 Cambodians when it captured the isolated Paet Um camp.

2. While the separation of civilian and military elements of the border population has reduced the risk that the civilian camps will be directly attacked, they remain dangerously vulnerable to spillover fighting. This point was tragically underscored by the above-noted shelling of Site Two North on January 26, 1987, and also by another attack on January 12, 1987, when Vietnamese artillery and mortar shells landed in the vicinity of Site Eight, a civilian encampment. The shells came close enough to damage the camp's fence, and caused panic among its 30,000 residents.

3. While evacuation sites lie ready in the event of an attack, even they typically are located within the range of Vietnamese artillery fire, sometimes necessitating further relocations. A range of other security risks attend the evacuation process itself, including the possibility of encountering land mines.

4. The Lawyers Committee recommends that the settlements for displaced Cambodians be moved further away from the border, and believes that the security of those residents would thereby be greatly enhanced. By establishing new sites beyond the range of Vietnamese artillery fire, Thailand would enable the Cambodian border population to live in reasonably stable, secure locations until conditions permit a permanent solution to their situation.

14

Violence Perpetrated by Cambodians

5. Cambodians living on the Thai-Cambodian border are also vulnerable to attack by other Cambodians, often in connection with smuggling or black-market activities. Gangs of armed Cambodians, widely referred to as "bandits," have terrorized Khao I Dang, Site Two and other camps in the past two years. Thai villages have been similarly victimized. Armed with automatic weapons and rocket-propelled grenade guns, the bandits typically strike at night, sometimes in groups as large as 30.

6. Many of these bandits apparently are deserters from the Khmer People's National Liberation Front (KPNLF), while others appear to be on active duty in KPNLF military units. KPNLF forces until recently under the command of Chea Chhut in particular have been implicated in bandit raids. Though enhanced security measures brought the banditry under control in Khao I Dang in April 1985, and in Site Two in October 1985, a spate of more recent incidents has underscored the need for renewed efforts to address the problem.

7. Although the Thai government has entrusted the KPNLF with primary responsibility for maintaining law and order in civilian encampments affiliated with the Front, the Lawyers Committee believes that Thailand must be prepared to assume ultimate responsibility for the protection of the displaced Cambodians as long as they remain in Thailand. Consistent with its desire to promote more effective governance within the Khmer administration at Site Two, Thailand should be prepared to exercise there its general responsibility for law enforcement with respect to criminal behavior occurring in Thai territory.

8. Displaced Cambodians have been especially vulnerable to attack by other Cambodians before they reach Thailand, as they make their way to the border. Cambodians — as well as Vietnamese — fleeing their homelands have often been raped and robbed by guerrilla troops shortly before they reach the Thai border. Many of those who have been intercepted by these troops have been taken to sites on the border that are largely beyond the reach of international relief organizations. They have been detained there until relatives abroad send ransoms for their release.

9. Such depradations have occurred most often in the vicinity of Rithisen and Chamkar Ko, KPNLF military bases that, at least until recently, operated under the command of Liv Ne. While Liv Ne's troops appear to have been responsible for the bulk of these abuses, Khmer Rouge troops also have been implicated in rapes and robberies of Vietnamese and Cambodians near Rithisen. Similar abuses have been perpetrated by troops under the command of Chea Chhut, who, at least until recently, was the commander of the KPNLF military base known as Nong Chan.

10. A series of measures were undertaken to address these abuses in late 1986. On October 25, 1986, the ICRC and UNBRO moved over 1000 civilians out of Rithisen, Chamkar Ko and Nong Chan and into Site Two, where they are under the protective eye of the international humanitarian organizations that provide assistance to that camp. In late November, the Chief of Staff of the Royal Thai Army met with KPNLF military leaders, and made it clear that the abuses must end. The KPNLF claims that it has transferred Liv Ne and Chea Chhut away from the bases they formerly commanded, along with most of the troops there, and that it has left in place only enough troops to guard the entry points to Thailand. It also claims to have established procedures to investigate and discipline abusive troops. While it remains to be seen how effective these measures will be in ending the abuses, the Lawyers Committee welcomes them as an indication that the responsible authorities recognize the gravity of the situation, and are willing to act to address the abuses.

Abuses Committed by Thai Security Forces

11. A separate threat to the Cambodians is posed by the very paramilitary units that the Thai government has assigned to guard and protect them — the rangers who staff Task Force 80, a unit established in 1980 to handle security matters pertaining to the displaced Cambodians. While many rangers have provided valuable security to the Cambodians — at times heroically — others have beaten, robbed, raped and reportedly even killed the camp residents.

12. Such actions typically have not received appropriate discipline by the Task Force 80 officers who command the rangers.

16

And, on at least one occasion, some Task Force 80 officers have themselves tortured Cambodians in Thailand. On the night of March 21-22, 1986, three Task Force 80 officers inflicted severe torture on three Cambodians who were arrested on suspicion of having participated in a violent raid in Khao I Dang. Their torture included having a hot iron and burning firewood applied to various parts of their bodies; having their hair set on fire; having boiling, salted water poured over their open wounds; and being whipped with electric cables. In subsequent interrogations, the three victims were subjected to mock executions.

13. Though it appears unlikely that the Task Force 80 officers who tortured the Cambodians will ever be held fully accountable for their abuses, recent developments have afforded some measure of relief — though not redress — to the victims of the torture. On December 18, 1986, a civilian court dismissed charges against the three victims, finding insufficient evidence to proceed with the prosecution. Then, in early January, the three were granted asylum in Sweden.

14. The Lawyers Committee believes that the behavior of the Thai rangers warrants a change in the practices utilized to recruit them, as well as more vigorous discipline when abuses are committed. We support a reform now under consideration by Task Force 80 to recruit rangers from reservists in the Royal Thai Army. We believe that the training and discipline of such reservists would be far superior to that of the average ranger who now serves on the border.

15. The Lawyers Committee also believes that information regarding actions taken to discipline abusive rangers should be made available to officials of the international relief organizations that play a protection role vis-a-vis the displaced Cambodians. Such independent monitoring would strengthen Thailand's efforts to improve ranger discipline.

Khmer Rouge Control of Civilians

16. Special concerns are raised by the control by Khmer Rouge forces of some 59,000 Cambodians living in camps in Thailand. Remnants of a regime responsible for the deaths of at least one million of Cambodia's total population of seven million, the Khmer Rouge today exert rigid control over the lives of these civilians. Such control includes frequent admonitions by the Khmer Rouge administrators of Site Eight, which holds over 30,000 civilians, that the camp residents will be punished if they express discontent to relief workers or other "foreigners."

17. Pervasive intimidation of those civilians has at times been reinforced by removal of some of them to the Khmer Rouge logistics base at Phnom Dey, where they reportedly must undergo "re-education." Such punitive transfers to Phnom Dey, which is beyond the protective reach of international relief organizations, have apparently been tolerated by Thai authorities. From Phnom Dey, some of these civilians are reportedly pressed into the hazardous duty of transporting military supplies to Khmer Rouge guerrillas operating in the interior of Cambodia.

18. Particularly vulnerable to punitive transfers to Phnom Dey, as well as the Cambodian interior, are persons who express a desire to live in one of the non-communist camps affiliated with the KPNLF or FUNCINPEC. It is commonly estimated that at least one-third of Site Eight's 30,000 residents would move to such camps if given the opportunity.

19. Although displaced persons typically do not have the right to determine where, in a host country, they will live, the Lawyers Committee believes that humanitarian considerations justify an exception with respect to those wishing to free themselves of the grasp of Khmer Rouge forces. In this respect, it is significant that the top leadership of the Khmer Rouge today still consists of many of the same people who held leadership positions during the Khmer Rouge's period of genocidal rule in the late 1970's. Accordingly, the Lawyers Committee urges the Thai government to authorize UNBRO to assist civilians who wish to be transferred from Khmer Rouge-controlled camps to settlements affiliated with one of the non-communist groupings.

Removal of Cambodians in UNHCR-assisted
Facilities to the Border

20. Approximately 24,000 Cambodians who now enjoy the relative security afforded by greater distance from the border and by the UNHCR's protection mandate are to be removed to sites close to the border, with all their attendant risks. These are the Cambodians who live in the UNHCR-assisted Khao I Dang holding center and its Annex. On December 29, 1986, the Thai government announced that those facilities would be closed two days later, and that their residents subsequently would be moved to existing camps along the border.

21. The Lawyers Committee opposes the relocation of these populations to the existing border encampments on security grounds. To do so would merely enlarge the number of persons who are already endangered by the brooding threat of attack posed by hostile armed forces poised on the other side of the border. Additionally, removal of the Khao I Dang/Annex populations to the border settlements could place them in the midst of a hostile population. Those living in Khao I Dang and its Annex are perceived by many Cambodians on the border as having "voted with their feet" not to support the guerrilla groupings to which the border settlements are linked.

22. Accordingly, the Lawyers Committee recommends that the current residents of Khao I Dang and its Annex be given the option of being relocated to a new location separate from the border settlements and further away from the border than those settlements — in short, to a safe, neutral location. Additionally, we strongly recommend that the UNHCR retain jurisdiction over the current residents of Khao I Dang and the Annex wherever they are relocated.

Strengthening International Protection

23. The Lawyers Committee further recommends that the protection mandate of the UNHCR be extended to encompass the entire population of displaced Cambodians in Thailand. Despite the multiple and substantial security threats faced by the border camp residents, none of the international organizations providing

assistance to them plays a comprehensive protection role. While any of the three major humanitarian organizations operating in Thailand — UNBRO, the ICRC or the UNHCR — conceivably could serve this function, the UNHCR may be the most appropriate of the three to do so. It has an explicit protection mandate, as well as considerable expertise in implementing that mandate in troubled regions throughout the world.

24. Many of the abuses in camps along the border occur at night, when there is no international relief presence. Stationing international personnel in the larger camps at night would enhance the residents' security, particularly if such personnel were equipped with radios by which they could communicate with Task Force 80 personnel.

25. The security situation of the displaced Cambodians in Thailand merits the concerted attention of the international community. To ensure that this issue receives greater attention, detailed reports on the security situation should be regularly prepared — at least semi-annually — under the auspices of the United Nations humanitarian assistance program. These reports should be circulated among foreign embassies in Bangkok, at the meetings of representatives of nations that fund the relief program in Thailand, at the foreign ministries in the capitals of those nations, and at the headquarters of private voluntary agencies involved in the relief effort there.

26. As a close ally of Thailand, the United States can and should play a key role in promoting the protection of displaced Cambodians. Until recently, it largely failed to exercise that influence. Its recent initiative in promoting the security of the displaced Cambodians in Thailand has surely played a significant part in promoting greater attention to this issue by responsible Thai officials. Its continued and sustained attention to these issues are, just as surely, necessary to ensure that the problems are adequately addressed.

II. THE ROOTS OF THE CAMBODIAN PRESENCE IN THAILAND

The vast majority of displaced Cambodians now living in Thailand took refuge there from a Vietnamese military offensive, of unprecedented scale, that was launched at the end of 1984. Directed against encampments of Cambodian guerrillas opposed to the Vietnamese-backed government in Phnom Penh, the 1984-85 offensive pushed some 230,000 Cambodian civilians out of the adjacent settlements they had occupied inside Cambodia across the border and into Thailand.

A. Spillover from the War in Indochina

Their flight to Thailand was preceded by two decades of extraordinary turmoil. It began in the mid-1960's, when Prince Norodom Sihanouk's Kingdom of Cambodia sought to maintain a neutralist stance as the war in Indochina increasingly spilled over into the eastern part of the country, and an internal political crisis brewed. Prince Sihanouk's inability to keep the war out of Cambodia set the stage for his downfall in a coup that brought to power his chief military adviser, General Lon Nol, in March 1970.[1]

The following years brought mounting destruction. Local communist insurgents led by Pol Pot, who claimed alliance with the deposed Prince Sihanouk and were supported by North Vietnam and China, waged an increasingly fierce war against the United States-backed government of Lon Nol. From 1970 through 1973, intense U.S. bombing aimed at wiping out both Vietnamese bases in eastern Cambodia and the growing insurgency devastated the

---

1. In the early 1960's Vietnamese communist forces, seeking, at least in part, to evade attack by U.S. forces in southern Vietnam, established sanctuaries in Cambodia. Prince Sihanouk acquiesced in their establishment and permitted North Vietnam's allies to use the Cambodian port of Sihanoukville to supply North Vietnam's units in South Vietnam. The United States secretly bombed the sanctuaries. In 1970 General Nol seized power in a coup by military forces supported by Cambodians who hoped to drive the Vietnamese out of Cambodia.

countryside.[2] By early 1972, two million Cambodians were homeless because of the fighting.[3] By one estimate, the war had claimed some 450,000 Cambodian casualties[4] by the time the insurgents — an indigenous communist group that Prince Sihanouk had dubbed "les Khmer rouges" ("the red Khmer") — emerged victorious and proclaimed the birth of Democratic Kampuchea in April 1975.

B. The Victory of the Khmer Rouge

On April 17, 1975, Khmer Rouge troops entered Phnom Penh. Within days, they evacuated virtually the entire war-swollen population of the city — about 2.5 million people. Ordinary urban life was abolished, as the Khmer Rouge began to implement with murderous impact a radical social ideology that sought to transform the entire nation into agricultural and industrial producers. Brutally executed, the first step in this transformation was a forced march of the urban evacuees into the countryside. Many of the Khmer Rouge cadres who supervised the exodus took no pity on the aged or infirm, and thousands died along the way.

But the worst was yet to come. The urban evacuees and other Cambodians relocated by the new government were made to work, mainly in agricultural teams that cultivated rice, under slavish conditions. They often labored seven days a week under the merciless supervision of Khmer Rouge cadres, who doled out daily rations consisting of little more than a handful of rice. Many died of starvation or exhaustion. Others were barbarously executed by Khmer Rouge cadres. Families were torn apart as children were taken away to labor in age-linked work brigades. Because of Khmer Rouge policy, almost no medicine was available to those who fell ill, and illnesses that would have been manageable with proper rest, food and treatment instead proved fatal.

---

2. For a detailed account of this period, see William Shawcross, *Sideshow* (1979).

3. *Id.* at 399, citing a February 5, 1972 figure reported by the Refugee Subcommittee of the U.S. Senate Judiciary Committee.

4. Joel Charney and John Spragens, Jr., *Obstacles to Recovery in Vietnam and Kampuchea* (1984) at 78.

Some Cambodians were singled out for especially harsh treatment. Those suspected of having been soldiers under Lon Nol's government were often imprisoned or executed. In some areas, inadvertently revealing one's middle-class background — by wearing eyeglasses or having good teeth or a certain manner of speaking — could draw brutal torture, and even summary execution.

All told, at least one million of Cambodia's total population of seven million died of starvation, disease, punishment or outright execution during the years of Khmer Rouge rule.

C. The Vietnamese Invasion

The nightmare abated with the December 1978 invasion of Cambodia by Vietnamese troops.[5] The Vietnamese installed Heng Samrin, a former Khmer Rouge military commander who had been purged by Pol Pot after losing battles to the Vietnamese, as the titular head of the newly formed People's Republic of Kampuchea (PRK).

The months following the invasion by Vietnam saw a mass flow of Cambodians to the Thai border. Many fled because the fall of the Democratic Kampuchea regime created the first opportunity for Cambodians to escape a country that had become a living hell. Few had been able to flee to Thailand while the Khmer Rouge ruled Cambodia. [6] The flow intensified in April and May of 1979, as tens

---

5. The conflict between the Democratic Kampuchea regime and North Vietnam had an international dimension. By the time of the Vietnamese invasion, the former had established strong ties with China, while Vietnam had become estranged from China and linked to the Soviet Union.

6. From April 1975 through December 1978, only a relative trickle of 34,000 managed to cross into Thailand. United States Committee for Refugees, *Cambodians in Thailand: People on the Edge* (December 1985) at 7. A considerably larger number had gone to Vietnam during the same period, often in the course of border fighting: at least 320,000 persons — over half of them ethnic Vietnamese — made their way to Vietnam. Milton Osborne, "The Indo-Chinese Refugee Situation: A Kampuchea Case Study," *Proceedings of the Fourth Symposium of the Academy of the Social Sciences in Australia* (1980) at 36 n.3.

of thousands of Cambodians sought to locate their surviving relatives, and came to realize that their pre-Pol Pot lives had ceased to exist.

Others left to avoid policies implemented by the new regime or policies they feared it might adopt in the future. First to be affected by the Vietnamese occupation were merchants concerned about controls on trade, newly re-established urban inhabitants fearing the prospect of another round of forced relocations to the countryside, and ethnic Chinese suffering discrimination at the hands of the Vietnamese.

Still others, including large numbers of peasants, fled from food shortages and a perceived likelihood of famine. Between July and October of 1979, hundreds of thousands flowed to the border to escape the looming spectre of famine.

Some decided to join or organize armed opposition movements to the new regime from bases near the Thai border. With varying degrees of voluntariness, many civilians who went to the border came to live in areas under the control of those forces.

Non-communist movements opposing the Vietnamese presence in Cambodia, some of which had previously fought the Khmer Rouge, were fielding armed forces along the Thai border within months of the invasion. In October 1979, several of them merged under the leadership of former Prime Minister Son Sann,[7] forming the Khmer People's National Liberation Front (KPNLF). Others joined it later. During 1981, still other movements formed a second grouping, the National United Front for an Independent, Peaceful and Cooperative Cambodia (known by its French acronym, FUNCINPEC), which took shape along the border under the titular leadership of Prince Sihanouk.

Driven from Phnom Penh and most of the countryside, Khmer Rouge forces retreated to areas bordering Thailand and, by 1980,

---

7. Son Sann served as Prime Minister under Prince Norodom Sihanouk in the 1960's. Because of disagreements with Prince Sihanouk, Son Sann went into exile in Paris in the late 1960's, and he remained there until 1979.

once again began to operate as a guerrilla force. They brought with them several hundred thousand civilians, many of whom were violently forced to join evacuation columns guarded by Khmer Rouge troops. A Vietnamese offensive against Khmer Rouge positions west of Battambang in April 1979 drove tens of thousands of these civilians, along with Khmer Rouge troops, still closer to or across the border.

Despite their strong animosities toward the Khmer Rouge, the two non-communist groupings, responding to foreign pressure, joined their former enemy in the Coalition Government of Democratic Kampuchea (CGDK) in 1982.[8] While the coalition parties jointly oppose the Vietnamese presence in Cambodia, each maintains control over distinct civilian populations. Today, virtually every Cambodian living along the Thai border is in a settlement administered by one of the three guerrilla forces.[9]

D. Exodus in Thailand

Thailand has been a country of first asylum for hundreds of thousands of Southeast Asian refugees since 1945. Though generally unwilling to accept such refugees as permanent residents, Thailand, which has enjoyed peace since World War II, has generously offered temporary refuge to the battered victims of her war-torn neighbors.

The Thai government had a special interest in supporting the Cambodians streaming to the border in the wake of Vietnam's invasion. With the Vietnamese occupation of Cambodia, Thailand had

---

8. With United States backing, China, Singapore and Thailand were the main proponents of the coalition. The coalition is the government of the state of Democratic Kampuchea, which today holds Cambodia's seat at the United Nations.

9. In late 1985, long-simmering tensions led to a fissure within the KPNLF, which continues to the present day. Perhaps the majority of key military commanders, and a number of important civilian administrators in Site Two, are loyal to the dissident faction, which opposes certain policies of KPNLF President Son Sann.

lost the buffer that had previously stood between it and Vietnam. Encouraged by China and with U.S. acquiescence, Thailand adopted the policy of encouraging the growth of guerrilla groups opposed to the Vietnamese-backed government in Phnom Penh along the border it shares with Cambodia.[10]

In doing so, Thailand had not foreseen the massive strain on its resources threatened by the unprecedented influx of Cambodians — as well as Vietnamese — in early 1979. Alarmed by the overwhelming scale of new refugees from Indochina, Thai officials resorted to severe measures to stem the flood of aliens. A series of forced and violent repatriations of Cambodians culminated on June 8, 1979, when some 43,000 were bussed from camps in eastern Thailand to Preah Vihear on the northeastern border with Cambodia, and were forced at gunpoint to stumble down a mine-strewn mountainside. Thousands were maimed or killed.

The Thai action provoked an international outcry. The international attention that Thailand's drastic measures drew ultimately produced a commitment by other nations to share the burden of assisting Cambodians displaced by their nation's upheavals. At the Foreign Ministers' meeting of the Association of Southeast Asian Nations shortly after the Preah Vihear incident, U.S. Secretary of State Cyrus Vance promised the Thai government that the United States would help arrange international support for Cambodians fleeing to Thailand, and that it would also be generous in resettling those Cambodians. Seeking to revive Thailand's willingness to afford first asylum, other Western nations and the United Nations High Commissioner for Refugees offered similar assurances. The combined pressure and promises of support from other countries and organizations induced Thailand to adopt a more generous policy toward the Cambodians streaming out of their country, and Cambodians collected at the border in greater numbers than before.

The resolve of Thailand and other nations alike was tested in subsequent months, when increasingly alienating Vietnamese

---

10. See William Shawcross, *The Quality of Mercy*, 79-80 (1984).

policies, a fear of famine inside Cambodia and the westward push of the Vietnamese Army combined to produce a flow of well over 500,000 persons to the border by October 1979. Most collected at a series of camps east of the Thai border town of Aranyaprathet. The Khmer Rouge retained control of a portion of that population, settling them in sites named Phnom Chhat, Nong Pru and Ta Prik.[11] The majority, however, made their way to the border on their own, and ended up in sites controlled by armed non-communist elements that had cleared mines and made promises to provide food. The main camps — Mak Moun, Nong Samet and Nong Chan — were dominated by "warlords"[12] who were motivated by varying degrees of devotion to fighting the Vietnamese and profiteering from taxation of trade.

Residents of both the Khmer Rouge and non-communist camps received desperately needed food, which eventually was supplied jointly by the International Committee of the Red Cross (ICRC) and the United Nations Children's Fund (UNICEF). In addition, the ICRC and UNICEF subsequently utilized Nong Chan and Phnom Chhat as "land bridges," emergency transfer points at which Cambodians remaining in their country came to receive food and medicine, which they took back to their families in their country's interior.

In late 1979, the Thai government decided to grant some Cambodians temporary asylum slightly farther inside Thailand and off the border, in camps administered by the Thai government and supported by the United Nations High Commissioner for Refugees (UNHCR).[13] Starting on October 24, 30,000 Khmer Rouge cadres,

---

11. The Khmer Rouge also herded civilians to military bases to the south of the sites named.

12. See Chapter IV, *infra*. See also Lawyers Committee for Human Rights, *Kampuchea: After the Worst* (August 1985) at 215.

13. Previously, the Thai government had allowed Khmer Rouge cadres and combatants — and persons under their control — refuge at a camp called Khao Laan, but international access was severely limited. Many of these were returned to the border after a couple of months.

soldiers and civilians whom they had controlled were taken to a site that became the Sakeo Holding Center. On November 21 the Thai government opened Khao I Dang Holding Center for Cambodians not under Khmer Rouge control. This change in Thai policy stemmed from the combination of pressure and promises from UNHCR and Western nations, to the effect that the holding centers would only be temporary and that their Cambodian residents would be voluntarily repatriated to Cambodia or resettled abroad. Though Thailand officially closed Khao I Dang to new arrivals on January 15, 1980, thousands of Cambodians have been able to enter the camp surreptitiously since then. Its population peaked at 140,000 in June 1980, after which returns to the border and third-country resettlement gradually drew down the total.[14] In the next two years, other holding centers were opened and closed, eventually leaving Khao I Dang as the only such facility.[15] Though Khao I Dang itself was officially closed at the end of 1986, its population has not yet been moved elsewhere, and it appears that the process of doing so may be quite protracted.[16]

Some of the border population seeped back into the Cambodian interior in 1980, as conditions in their homeland stabilized, the food situation improved, and internecine fighting destroyed the largest camps. But about a quarter of a million remained along the border, just inside Cambodia. Many stayed for the same reasons they had fled in the first place: fear of famine or of the Vietnamese; a commitment to anti-Vietnamese opposition forces; the knowledge or

---

14. Over 200,000 Cambodians have been resettled abroad since 1979.

15. In November 1985, however, the Thai government established the Khao I Dang Annex, to hold 7,000 persons removed from Khao I Dang. These persons were ineligible to remain in Khao I Dang because they had entered the camp after an amnesty-like registration in August 1984 of persons previously unauthorized to be there. Like Khao I Dang, and unlike the border camps, the Annex is a UNHCR-supported facility. But unlike the Khao I Dang population, the Annex residents are barred by Thailand from consideration for resettlement abroad.

16. See Chapter VII, *infra*.

belief that their homes had been destroyed; and lack of choice, particularly with respect to those living under Khmer Rouge control.

With the exception of the Cambodians living in holding centers inside Thailand, the majority of the displaced Cambodians lived in areas that straddle the international frontier for most of the period from 1979 until 1984. Throughout that time, their residences were periodically disrupted by annual dry season offenses against the guerrilla bases by Vietnamese troops, sometimes forcing border residents into temporary evacuation sites clearly in Thailand. The residents of the KPNLF's Nong Chan camp, for example, have moved six times since early 1983, each new "home" initially consisting of a chaotic jumble of plastic sheets overhead and bare ground beneath them. (The more "permanent" huts, when they are constructed, consist of bamboo walls and thatch roofs.) Until 1985, the Vietnamese generally withdrew after such attacks, allowing the displaced persons to return either to the areas they had previously occupied along the border, or, at Thai insistence, to sites clearly inside Cambodia.

The pattern of flight and return was broken in late 1984/early 1985, when Vietnamese troops launched the largest and most successful of their annual offensives. Virtually the entire border population was driven well into Thailand, and then Vietnamese forces remained in the camps just inside Cambodia. In many places, they began building fortifications right up to the international frontier, hoping to stop guerrilla infiltration. The displaced Cambodians have since been allowed to remain in camps clearly inside Thailand, most of them adjacent to the border shared with Cambodia.

E. Administration of the Camps

Each of the border settlements is administered by personnel linked to one of the guerrilla groups opposing the Vietnam-backed regime in Phnom Penh. The daily administration of these camps is supervised by Cambodian civilian administrators who live in them. Almost all of these administrators answer directly to guerrilla commanders and, via them, to the political leaders of the opposition groups[17] with which their camps are affiliated. A few administrators, however, have some degree of autonomy.

Final control over major issues of camp administration and security matters resides with Task Force 80, a Thai security force established in 1980 to ensure the security of and supervise the displaced Cambodians on the border and in holding centers in Thailand.

Relief assistance to the border population is provided by the United Nations Border Relief Operation (UNBRO), created in 1982 to take over the relief services previously provided by UNICEF. A lean, efficient organization, UNBRO supplies water and basic rations to the border population, assists 80,000 Thai villagers whose lives have been disrupted by the Cambodian presence and fighting along the border, and coordinates a plethora of other relief activities, many of which are provided by various private relief organizations that operate under UNBRO's overall supervision. While malaria, other ailments and a limited degree of malnutrition are not uncommon in the camps, because of UNBRO's work the supply of food and medical care there is adequate and (except during evacuations) better than that found in many other regions where large populations of displaced persons have massed.

The holding center at Khao I Dang and its Annex are administered by the Thai government in cooperation with the United Nations High Commissioner for Refugees (UNHCR).[18] The

---

17. In the case of the KPNLF, it may be more accurate to say that the camp administrators ultimately answer to the leader of the faction to which they adhere. See note 9, *supra*.

18. UNBRO was created to assist the border population in part because the UNHCR declined to do so. A principal rationale had been that the UNHCR's mandate extends only to displaced persons who have gone "outside the country of [their] nationality" (paragraph 63 of the UNHCR Statute), and the Cambodian border population lived on the Cambodian side of the border until two years ago. In fact, however, the UNHCR can in theory exercise its "good offices" to assist persons who are internally displaced. In any case, the displaced Cambodians in Thailand now reside "outside the country of [their] nationality."

roughly 17,000 Cambodians now living in Khao I Dang consist primarily of persons considered for third-country resettlement and rejected. Another 7,000 Cambodians occupy the neighboring UNHCR-administered facility, the Khao I Dang Annex, to which they were moved by Thai authorities, from Khao I Dang itself, in November 1985. Having entered Khao I Dang illegally and after an amnesty-like registration of camp residents in 1984, the Annex population is barred by the Thai government from eligibility for resettlement abroad.

The UNBRO-assisted border population consists of 243,000 Cambodians, and 3,000 Vietnamese, spread among 13 camps along the border.[19] Some 59,000 Cambodians live in three camps in the hilly, northern border region; another 15,000 are in three camps in the south. Approximately 172,000 persons (including the 3,000 Vietnamese) are in the relatively flat central zone's seven camps. The bulk of this group, belonging to five KPNLF-affiliated camps and the one Vietnamese border camp, has been brought together by Thai authorities into the area UNBRO has designated Site Two.[20] Of the 243,000 Cambodians constituting the UNBRO-supported border population, some 146,000 live in six camps affiliated with the KPNLF, 59,000 live in five camps controlled by the Khmer Rouge, and 38,000 live in FUNCINPEC's one settlement, Site B.

While the location of most Cambodians now at Site Two was fixed in the first few months of 1985, the population of the largest camp, known as Nong Samet, was not fully established as Site Two South until September. Following Vietnam's attack on Christmas

---

19. As previously noted, figures pertaining to camp populations are derived from United Nations Border Relief Operation, *Situation Report as at August 15, 1986.* For a listing of the populations and CGDK affiliations of the border camps, see Appendix C.

20. Until recently Site Two also held approximately 200 Degas, members of a Montagnard hill tribe from Vietnam, who left their homes in 1980. They ended up at Site Two after living under Khmer Rouge control for an extended period. They have since been accepted for resettlement by the United States.

Day 1984, the Nong Samet population was evacuated to an interim location known as Red Hill, remaining there until January 20, 1985. It was then moved off the border to yet another interim home, designated by UNBRO as Site Seven. Site Seven was in fact situated next to Khao I Dang. With its return to the border, Nong Samet's population became part of Site Two's 141,000 displaced persons, constituting more than half of the border population and the largest concentration of displaced Cambodians since 1980.

F. Current Thai Policy Toward the Cambodians

Thailand's general policy toward the displaced Cambodians is the balance struck among a raft of fluid, diverse, and sometimes competing considerations. Thailand's support for the guerrilla coalition opposing the Vietnamese presence in Cambodia has disposed it to allow civilians linked with those guerrillas to remain on Thai soil until they can safely be resettled in Cambodia or a third country. At the same time (and often as a counterweight to such regional policy objectives) Thailand has, since the first large wave of Cambodians entered in 1979, sought to ensure that it does not become permanently burdened with the Cambodians and that its policies do not serve as a magnet for other Cambodians who have not yet fled their country.[21] In this regard, the Thai government has evinced understandable concern over the years that, as the international community's attention toward the displaced Cambodians

---

21. Also feeding into the policy-formulation process are Thailand's concerns that the Cambodian presence along the border may endanger Thai villages, and engender domestic political tensions, ethnic hostility and local economic dislocations. Programs relating to the international relief effort on the border have sought to address some of these concerns. The international community covers the costs of the bulk of the relief effort — UNBRO alone spends close to 40 million dollars per year — on programs that generate a ripple effect benefiting the Thai economy. Foreign exchange, infrastructure development, and local employment and business all have benefited from the activities of the United Nation's Kampuchean Humanitarian Assistance Programs. Some 80,000 Thai villagers affected by the Cambodian presence benefit from U.N. assistance.

wanes, Thailand will be left shouldering the burden of absorbing them — and the costs of their support.[22]

Such concerns lie behind Thailand's general policy of "humane deterrence" toward the Cambodians, reflected, for example, in its 1980 decision to close its borders to new Cambodians; to deny any new entrants legal status as refugees; and to deny them the right to be considered for third-country resettlement.[23] It has likewise led the Thai government to resist efforts to improve the educational programs available to residents of the Cambodian settlements on the border.[24] And, of particular importance to the security problems addressed in this report, such concerns appear to be a factor in Thailand's general unwillingness to allow the border population to be located deeper inland — further away from the security threat posed by the Vietnamese troops stationed just across the border.

Thailand has thus resisted recent entreaties by UNBRO, various private relief organizations, and some representatives of the U.S. government to move the border population further inland.[25] And, in the years before Vietnam's major offensive in 1984/85, the Thai government consistently refused to allow Cambodians to remain indefinitely on Thai soil following military offensives that drove them into temporary evacuation sites in Thailand. As noted earlier,

---

22. In a meeting of the Committee for the Coordination of Services to Displaced Persons in Thailand (CCSDPT) on October 10, 1986, Khachadpai Burusapatana, the Deputy Secretary General of Thailand's National Security Council, said that the decrease in the number of refugees settled in third countries raised concerns that the international community might be forgetting its responsibilities. He also stated that there were only two solutions to the refugee problem in Thailand that were compatible with the situation there and acceptable to the Thai government: third-country resettlement and voluntary repatriation. CCSDPT, Minutes of the Open Session (October 10, 1986).

23. See Chapter VII, *infra*.

24. See United States Department of State, *Report of the Indochinese Refugee Panel* (April 1986) at 30; Refugees International, *The Dilemma of Khmer in Thailand: An Opportunity for Action* (September 1986).

25. See United States Department of State, *Report of the Indochinese Refugee Panel* (April 1986) at 29.

the residents of such evacuation sites were forced to return to sites clearly on the Cambodian side of the border once Vietnamese troops retreated.

In short, while several factors animate Thai policy regarding the very presence and location of the Cambodians — including concerns about drawing Vietnamese fire against Thai villages — an important factor appears to be Thailand's desire to maintain the visibility of the plight of the Cambodians for the international community. In doing so, it hopes to ensure that the world does not turn its attention entirely elsewhere while Thailand remains burdened with an alien and increasingly static population.[26]

While any report examining the security situation of the displaced Cambodians in Thailand will necessarily fault various aspects of Thai policy, the most salient aspect of that policy remains Thailand's unmatched generosity as a country of first asylum for displaced Indochinese. Today, Thailand's population is swollen with literally hundreds of thousands of Indochinese displaced by the region's political upheavals.

Thailand's current practice in this regard is also its historical practice. In 1954, for example, after the fall of the colonial government in Vietnam, Thailand received a mass exodus of Vietnamese, and since then has absorbed significantly more. For some decades, Thailand has shared in the unending costs of wars not of its own making. For this, it deserves both understanding and appreciation, even as it is criticized for its failure adequately to assure the security of those to whom it has provided refuge.

---

26. In this, Thailand's concern is grounded on more than hypothetical apprehensions. In recent years, third-country resettlement has declined markedly, as Cambodians most clearly eligible for resettlement have completed the resettlement process, and financial support for the international relief effort has also fallen off.

III. THAI RANGERS AND TASK FORCE 80

The principal responsibility for protecting the Cambodians in Thailand from attacks against their physical security lies with Task Force 80, a Thai military unit created in 1980 to supervise and provide security to the Cambodians in Thailand and on the border, and to the paramilitary "ranger" troops that operate under its command. While many rangers have provided valuable security to the Cambodians — at times heroically — others have beaten, robbed, raped, and reportedly even killed the camp residents.

Such actions typically do not receive appropriate discipline by the Task Force 80 officers who command the rangers. And, on one occasion, several Task Force 80 officers themselves tortured Cambodians in Thailand.

A. The Rangers

Ranger units perform a variety of functions in Thailand, many wholly unrelated to the camps. They originally were formed as village-based defense forces to suppress the communist insurgency that was most active in the country's border areas in the 1970's. Despite the possible connotations of their name, the rangers are by no means an elite force. They are not even regular soldiers of the Royal Thai Army (RTA). Their pay, training and discipline are, in fact, inferior to that of regular RTA troops.

Officers from various units staff Task Force 80, while rangers constitute most of its troops. The jurisdiction of Task Force 80 includes Khao I Dang and the central border area camps, which contain the bulk of the Cambodian population. In the northern and southern border zones it shares responsibility with other Thai military units.

The caliber of ranger units varies widely. Some have heroically defended Cambodian camps from raids by Cambodian bandits.[1]

---

1. For discussion of this type of security threat, see Chapter IV, *infra.*

Several rangers have been wounded, and at least two killed, while defending Cambodians against such raids.

All too often, however, ranger units are ill-disciplined, unruly, and even violent. Some relief workers suspect that many ranger units include juvenile delinquents and paroled convicts. A score of press reports about rangers elsewhere in Thailand over the past five years recount incidents of criminal conduct against other Thais by rangers, often when inebriated. These include such violent acts by rangers as killing five people and wounding 20 others by throwing a hand grenade, while inebriated, at a temple fair,[2] and killing another ranger over an argument about jointly-stolen property.[3]

Violent actions by rangers against Cambodian camp dwellers typically occur when the latter violate rules established by Task Force 80. These include rules prohibiting residents from trading with Thai villagers, wandering outside a camp fence or — particularly with respect to Khao I Dang — seeking to enter a camp illegally. Although bribes often buy the rangers' indulgence of such infractions, these acts have at times drawn violent responses.

In many cases camp residents do not realize that their behavior may provoke punishment, or they surmise that their behavior will elicit only mild rebuke. They are sometimes punished, even severely, for "infractions" of rules that were never officially promulgated, or only sporadically enforced. Such behavior as trading at a camp fence with local Thais may be condoned for days or weeks, for example, leading camp residents to believe the practice is permitted, until one of them is beaten when caught trading.

A 15-year-old girl named Hem Saroun (P) committed such a violation in late September 1985. Her "punishment" was rape. She had gone outside the perimeter of Site Two to get water, apparently because the water tanks in her residential area were temporarily empty. A Thai ranger brandishing an M-16 rifle forced her,

---

2. *Bangkok Post* (January 17, 1985).

3. *Bangkok Post* (November 4, 1983). For synopsis of other press accounts of ranger abuses, see Appendix A.

another girl, a boy in his mid-teens and a man in his 20's to move farther away from the fence. When the four did not comply with the ranger's demand that they perform sexual acts, he raped Hem[4] after forcing the other three to lie in a shallow, muddy pond. Before allowing the four to leave, the rangers struck the boy and the man a few times each with a long stick.[5]

Chuon Pat (P) was struck by a spear because she attempted to trade with local Thais. One morning in late October 1985, Chuon was standing near a fence surrounding Site Two when Thai traders selling vegetables entered the camp. As she waited to see whether any more would approach, three rangers appeared outside the camp and ran toward the fence. The crowd scattered, but Chuon was slower than the others, and a rough wooden spear that a soldier tossed from a few meters away pierced her upper arm. Chuon's account was corroborated by hospital records, as well as a gash on her upper arm that was deep enough to expose her bone.[6] Several Site Two residents claimed that such spearing attacks by rangers are not uncommon.

Yok Khlang (P) also was assaulted after attempting to trade with a Thai. One afternoon in early November 1985, he arranged the future purchase of sugar and vegetables from a Thai woman. She insisted that Yok show her his home, so that she could find him if he did not later return to complete the transaction. As the two approached Yok's hut, three rangers ran up, grabbed Yok by the throat, and dragged him hundreds of feet back to the camp fence, kicking and striking him along the way. When they got Yok to a tree near the fence, the rangers repeatedly sought to knee him in the

---

4. In referring to this victim as "Hem," we follow the Cambodian practice of putting the family name before the given name. As previously noted, "(P)" denotes a pseudonym used to protect the identity of a victim.

5. Hem's version of the incident was corroborated by two of the other individuals involved, each of whom was interviewed separately.

6. A few days after the attack several persons in the market area confirmed that a woman Chuon's age had been struck by a spear thrown by a Thai soldier. An interview with another camp resident corroborated the details of her story.

chest (though the blows actually struck his arms, which he was using to cover his chest). One ranger then kicked Yok in the forehead, causing him momentarily to lose consciousness. According to witnesses, the rangers then prodded Yok back to consciousness with a stick. Summoning a Thai trader to interpret, the rangers asked whether Yok "was the one who had run off with two Thai women and kept them here." He denied this (and later told the Lawyers Committee that he did not know what the rangers were talking about). After a brief interrogation, the rangers kicked Yok again before releasing him.

The Lawyers Committee interviewed Yok the following day, and observed that his left forearm and forehead were badly bruised. Five witnesses corroborated the details of his account. Recalling the attack, they asserted: "This happens all the time." Indeed, reliable sources described similar incidents, which they had personally investigated.

Thai rangers have used extreme force in response to relatively minor infractions of camp regulations. In July 1985, for example, a Cambodian woman was wounded in the back by a grenade tossed by a ranger apparently because the woman was outside the fence surrounding Site Two. Similarly, in separate events in January 1985, two young Vietnamese persons at Site A, the temporary evacuation area for the Dong Ruk camp, were shot and killed by rangers, reportedly because they were outside the section of the camp set aside for Vietnamese.

Such attacks are at times misdirected, as well as excessive. This happened, for example, in October 1985 in Site Two, following a fight between a Vietnamese and a Cambodian. The Vietnamese reportedly had been serving as an informant for several rangers to help them determine which Cambodians' homes were worth robbing. He left the fight scene and returned with two of those rangers. The Cambodian with whom he had fought had already left, and the Vietnamese informant accused a different Cambodian of being the other brawler, perhaps because he resembled the first Cambodian in feature and in dress. The rangers beat the mis-identified man, and shot him in the shoulder.

Cambodians seeking to enter Khao I Dang illegally typically risk violent attack if caught by Thai rangers. Though Cambodians from the border camps or the interior of Cambodia frequently bribe their way past the rangers and into Khao I Dang, some have been shot while seeking entry there. This happened to six Cambodians in June 1985, as they arrived at the camp fence, accompanied by a Thai smuggler who had arranged their entry into Khao I Dang. Just as a ranger whom they had bribed was about to let them through the fence, a Task Force 80 officer appeared. Apparently fearing that he would be disciplined, the ranger panicked and opened fire with his automatic weapon. The six Cambodians and the Thai smuggler were killed.

A few weeks later, an unarmed KPNLF soldier tried to sneak into Khao I Dang to visit his family in neighboring Site Seven. A group of rangers caught him, and beat him until he was unconscious. They then dragged the soldier around the camp perimeter, finally taking him to the camp prison, where they realized that his injuries from the beating required hospitalization. He died that night.

Another unarmed soldier, Pok Chia (P), was robbed and beaten severely with rifle butts by rangers when he was caught trying to enter Site Two in mid-October 1985. When the Lawyers Committee interviewed Pok two weeks later, his arm was in a sling, one hand was badly swollen, and his breathing appeared strained and coughing painful due to injured ribs.

Several casualties ensued when the rangers conducted a sweep of Khao I Dang on February 17, 1985, in search of persons who were there illegally. One man was shot dead as he sought to flee the round-up. A 16-year-old girl was so frightened of being caught that she baked while hiding inside an empty steel water tank exposed to the tropical sun, and died of hypothermia. Several others who tried to hide were caught and beaten.

As recently as November 18, 1986, an illegal entrant who had been hiding in Khao I Dang was apprehended by several rangers. He was fatally shot at close range in the back of the head, and a post-mortem examination identified a bullet hole in his wrist which seemed to indicate that the victim's hands were behind his head when the fatal bullet was fired. Bruises covering his face indicated that the victim had been severely beaten before he was shot.

The rangers have reportedly provided two conflicting accounts of this incident. One version is that the victim was shot while trying to escape; the other is that he was wielding an axe, provoking the shooting as an act of self-defense. Neither account is consistent with the findings of the post-mortem examination.

Resisting the rangers' authority typically invites a violent attack, as exemplified during a ranger raid on a Site Two cockfight in mid-October 1985. A young man who fought back when beaten by rangers was struck in the head by a hatchet. According to several unconfirmed reports he died from the blow. During the same raid, a bystander was beaten into unconsciousness by rangers.

In the Site Seven market in July 1985, several Cambodian residents beat a ranger who was out of uniform (and whom they reportedly mistook for a Cambodian) because he snatched some cigarettes. The ranger soon returned with a few other rangers, who assaulted several residents and ravaged the marketplace.

Many ranger abuses bear no relation to violations of camp rules. Rangers on the prey often saunter through the camps — particularly Site Two North at the time of the Lawyers Committee's first visit[7] — out of uniform, a knife or hatchet sticking menacingly out of the back of their shorts. The Lawyers Committee interviewed several Cambodians who were robbed by such persons in broad daylight. One relief worker described an incident in which rangers carted off the clothes of residents in a wheelbarrow. It is not uncommon for

---

7. During the Committee's visit in January 1987, we were told by one informed observer that fatalities attributed to Thai rangers occur at similar rates *per capita* at Sites Two and Eight. Another observer stated that ranger abuses at Site Two still are concentrated at Site Two North.

40

rangers to poke their heads into huts in the camps, sometimes without any pretext for doing so, in search of goods or women. On two consecutive nights in mid-October 1985, two rangers — one armed with a gun, the other with a knife — rummaged through more than 20 huts in Site Two. One resident was slashed across the hand when he tried to keep them out of his home.

At times ranger violence is an unintended effect of poor training. Shortly after going to bed on March 30, 1985, four-year-old Thith Vuthy (P) was struck by a machine-gun bullet, which pierced her wrist and chest, and lodged in her neck. Task Force 80 rangers were training that evening, and had set up their targets just outside Site Seven (next to Khao I Dang), where the girl and her family were living before they were moved to Site Two South. Medical records confirmed her injury,[8] and suggested that at least two other Site Seven residents received bullet wounds in the course of the target practice, one in the head and the other in the leg.

B. Discipline for Ranger Abuses

Undoubtedly contributing to the rangers' abusive conduct is the Thai officers' seeming tolerance of these abuses. No person interviewed by the Lawyers Committee during its October 1985 visit was aware of any disciplinary measures for such conduct beyond a possible transfer or dismissal. According to one report, after two rangers robbed several homes, beat up a Cambodian who resisted the robbery, and threatened the life of another, their commanding officer merely ordered them to run circles around a flag pole.

During the Committee's October 1985 visit to Thailand, the Director of the Thai Command Center for the Relief of Kampucheans told the Committee's delegate that rangers caught creating problems are dismissed immediately, and added that they are dealt with "severely." He nonetheless trivialized their abusive behavior with

---

8. Mr. Golub, who observed a lump on the victim's neck, also saw an X-ray showing that a bullet was lodged there.

the explanation that "some young guys want to sow their wild oats."

Both the Chief of Staff of the Royal Thai Army, General Wanchai Ruangtrakul, and the then-Commander of Task Force 80, Col. Pao Pasant, told the Lawyers Committee during its January 1987 visit that there is an established procedure to investigate allegations of ranger abuse, and that those found guilty receive appropriate discipline. When a ranger abuse is reported, they explained, Col. Pao immediately appoints a committee to investigate the allegation. If wrongdoing is established, Gen. Wanchai told us, the violator receives "serious punishment." When asked what this entails, he replied: "Mostly, they're dismissed."[9] One of his deputies added that in the most serious cases, more severe punishment — by which he seemed to mean a term in prison — is meted out. In a separate interview with Col. Pao, we were told that at least ten rangers have been disciplined within the past year, though few of these rangers were criminally prosecuted[10] or detained. Instead, he told us, "Some are released from service. Some are transferred back to their parent unit for appropriate action," such as demotion.

Officials in the relief community whom we interviewed detected little evidence that rangers are disciplined, though apparently information regarding disciplinary action is not made available to them. There appears to be a general perception among informed observers in the relief community that Col. Pao typically has not disciplined abusive rangers, and that his predecessor imposed more discipline.

---

9. Interview by Floyd Abrams and Diane Orentlicher with Gen. Wanchai Ruangtrakul (January 8, 1987). In a comment reminiscent of the above-quoted comment made by the Director of the Thai Command Center for the Relief of Kampucheans one year earlier, a deputy to Gen. Wanchai added that there are a lot of ranger abuses because "there are a lot of Cambodian women around."

10. Col. Pao told us that rangers can be prosecuted before military courts for criminal conduct.

C. Proposed Efforts to Address Ranger Abuses

Perhaps because of this, at least in part, Col. Pao reportedly was replaced as Commander of Task Force 80 immediately after the Lawyers Committee's visit to Thailand in January 1987. Whatever the reasons for his replacement, the Committee believes that improved discipline of abusive rangers should be a high priority of his successor. We also believe that information regarding disciplinary measures should be made available, if only on a confidential basis, to officials of the international relief organizations that play a protection role vis-a-vis the displaced Cambodians.[11] Such independent monitoring would surely strengthen Thailand's efforts to improve ranger discipline.

But poor discipline is only one factor behind the proliferation of ranger abuse; effective control over ranger abuses must also include improved recruitment and training policies. In this regard, the Committee is encouraged by recent reports that the Thai government is considering possible reforms in its recruitment practices. One option apparently under consideration is to recruit all rangers from reservists in the Royal Thai Army.[12] Since such persons have been trained and served in the Army, their discipline and training would be markedly superior to that of current rangers.

D. Task Force 80 Officers

While most Thai abuses are carried out by rangers apparently acting on their own initiative, Task Force 80 officials have occasionally been implicated in violations as well. While far less frequent, these abuses have nonetheless been serious.

In May 1985 a relief worker saw a group of Cambodians in Site Eight beat another resident into unconsciousness while a Task Force 80 officer looked on. Both the victim and those beating him

---

11. For discussion of this subject, see Chapter VIII.B. *infra.*
12. According to Col. Pao, a relatively small number of current rangers were recruited from such reservists.

43

previously had been transferred to Site Eight from Khao I Dang as punishment.[13] The beating reportedly was triggered by the victim's escape from Site Eight and subsequent recapture. Reportedly to make an example of him, the officer threatened that the attackers would themselves be harmed unless they struck the victim. The relief worker's account was corroborated by the testimony of several other individuals.

In a highly publicized incident on the night of March 21-22, 1986, several Task Force 80 officers brutally tortured three Cambodians who lived in Khao I Dang and its Annex. The three victims, Nuon Sareuan, Kaev Mayoura and his younger brother Kaev Channa, all in their late teens or early twenties, were registered residents of Khao I Dang and the Annex.[14] It appears that the three, together with a fourth Cambodian, were arrested by Task Force 80 inside the Khao I Dang holding center during the day on March 21, on suspicion of having participated in a violent raid in Khao I Dang by unidentified Cambodians on March 17, 1986.[15] During that raid, one Task Force 80 soldier was killed, and another was wounded.[16]

While interrogated about this incident, the three Cambodians were subjected to severe torture. Amnesty International, the Nobel-prize winning human rights organization based in London, conducted an investigation into that torture that included interviews with the victims, observation of their scars and examination of

---

13. For discussion of this practice, see Chapter V, *infra*.

14. See Chapter VII, *infra*.

15. See Amnesty International, "Thailand: Torture of Three Kampuchean Nationals," AI Index: ASA 31/05/86 (July 1986) at 1.

16. *Id*. The Cambodians arrested on March 21 denied any participation in that raid, and in July 1986 Amnesty International reported that it had received reports that the three who were tortured were not involved in the incident. As noted below, charges against the three were dismissed by a civilian court on December 18, 1986, for insufficient evidence. Nevertheless, Amnesty International, which conducted an extensive investigation of the torture incident, believes that "initially at least, Task Force 80 suspected [the three torture victims] of being accomplices of the unidentified band of [Cambodians] who entered Khao I Dang Center during the night of 17-18 March and killed one Task Force 80 soldier and wounded another." *Id*. at 7.

medical records. Based upon this and other reliable information, Amnesty International concluded that "it appears to be confirmed beyond any reasonable doubt that the three were tortured by the application of a hot flat iron to various places on their bodies during the night of 21-22 March 1986 by an official of [Task Force 80] while in its custody. . . ."[17] Its conclusions were corroborated by the Lawyers Committee's investigation of this incident.

Amnesty International also concluded that "it appears beyond doubt" that Nuon Sareuan and Kaev Mayoura "were tortured by Task Force 80 officials who applied pieces of burning firewood to various parts of their bodies."[18] The two also alleged, in statements corroborated by others, that their hair was set on fire during the night of March 21-22, one by candles and the other with ignited gasoline.[19] That same night, Task Force 80 interrogators poured boiling, salted water over the open wounds produced by the application of the flat iron and the burning by firewood of the two. Finally, all three victims told Amnesty that "they were either whipped with electric cable, struck with automatic rifles or subjected to repeated kicking or stamping during the first night they were in Task Force 80 custody."[20]

The three were denied medical treatment for the next seven to eight days, during which they were held incommunicado in the Task Force 80 jail inside Khao I Dang. Two appear to have suffered permanent, crippling damage from the torture.[21]

Once the torture of the three Cambodians was publicized, they were subjected to several rounds of interrogation by Thai authorities, this time to discover "how information about their torture might have reached the outside world, and to compel or perhaps deceive them into making or signing confessions admitting to

---

17. *Id.* at 5.
18. *Id.*
19. *Id.* at 6.
20. *Id.*
21. See *id.*

alleged criminal offenses."[22] During the first round, the three were questioned by the same Task Force 80 official who had inflicted the most severe torture on the night of March 21-22. During the second session, conducted by that official and officials of the regular army, the three were told they would be summarily shot if they did not confess to involvement in robbery. The three were then subjected to mock executions, consisting of blindfolding the victims, leading each one outside, telling them they would be killed if they did not confess and firing shots over the heads of two of them. In the final round, the three were forced to sign documents in Thai which they did not understand. Upon signing them, the three were told by a Task Force 80 official that they were now "dead for sure."[23]

During the same session, the three were told clearly for the first time that they would be criminally tried. According to Amnesty International, the Task Force 80 official who conveyed this added that "Task Force 80 would ensure that the outcome of their trial would be certain punishment," and that, indeed, "they were being brought to trial in order to be punished," presumably for complaining about their torture to outsiders.[24] The same official, the victims told Amnesty International, told them that they were being brought to trial "so that Task Force 80 could 'score a victory' over the organizations that had tried to help them and that had in so doing given Task Force 80 a bad name, and that court punishment of them would also be a punishment of these organizations."[25]

---

22. *Id*. at 7. Responding publicly to the reports of torture, Thai officials denied that the three had been tortured, and asserted that they "had led to Khao I Dang camp a gang of criminals who robbed the refugees there on March 5 and 18," and killed one soldier and wounded several soldiers and refugees. *Bangkok Post* (July 9, 1986). Although Thai authorities claimed that the three Cambodians who were tortured had confessed to these crimes, the three denied having done so. See Amnesty International Report, *supra* note 15, at 7. A document filed by Thai authorities with a criminal court on June 5 refers only to an alleged offense committed on March 5-6, and makes no mention of the one on March 17-18 — the one they were interrogated about on the night of their arrest. See *id*. at 9.

23. *Id*. at 7-8.

24. *Id*. at 10.

25. *Id*.

While the eventual outcome of the trial proceedings belied these threats (see below), informed observers believed that it would be difficult for the three torture victims to receive a fair trial. In July 1986, Amnesty International publicized reports it had received to the effect that "potential defense witnesses in Khao I Dang Center have been subjected to a pattern of harassment and intimidation by Task Force 80 that is likely effectively to prevent them from feeling that it would be safe to give any testimony on behalf of the three."[26] More recently, the Lawyers Committee learned that one of the Task Force 80 officers who inflicted torture was returned to service at Khao I Dang, though he reportedly was subsequently transferred to Site B.

Such actions suggest that, far from disciplining the Task Force 80 officers who tortured the three Cambodians, high-level Thai authorities were complicit in efforts to shield them from accountability. Indeed, despite incontrovertible evidence that the three were tortured, Thailand's chief policy-maker with regard to the displaced Cambodians, Squadron Leader Prasong Soonsiri,[27] publicly absolved Task Force 80 of any wrongdoing. He claimed, according to press accounts, that an investigation he had ordered "showed that the conduct of the Thai soldiers in the case had been correct, proper and within their legal authority and responsibility, and they had not been involved in any torture."[28]

While thus protecting the Task Force 80 torturers, Prasong lashed out against Amnesty International for publicizing the abuses. He accused the organization of "interfering in Thailand's process of justice,"[29] and charged that its local affiliate — which he

---

26. *Id.* at 11.

27. At the time of these developments, Prasong, now Secretary General of the Office of the Prime Minister, was Secretary General of the National Security Council. Although his public actions with regard to this incident were irresponsible and, indeed, deplorable, the Lawyers Committee understands that Prasong has often been an effective advocate for constructive policies toward the displaced Cambodians in Thailand.

28. *Bangkok Post* (July 9, 1986).

29. *Id.*

incorrectly believed had supplied the International Secretariat with information regarding the March 21 torture incident — was infiltrated by communists.[30]

The most recent developments in this episode brought some measure of relief (though not redress) to the three torture victims. On December 18, 1986, the civilian court that was trying the three dismissed the charges against them on the ground that there was insufficient evidence to proceed with a prosecution. In early January 1987, the three were allowed to leave Thailand, having been granted asylum in Sweden.[31] While there is no indication that the Thai officers who tortured the three Cambodians will ever be properly disciplined for their actions, the dismissal of charges against the victims stands as a testament to the independence of Thailand's judiciary.

---

30. See *Bangkok Post* (July 12, 1986). In a recent meeting with Lawyers Committee representatives who were visiting the Thai-Cambodian border in connection with a study unrelated to the subject of this report, Major General Surin Vorathas, the Chief of Thailand's Command Center for the Relief of Kampucheans, said that no one from Amnesty International would be allowed in Thailand "as long as [he was] alive."

Though beyond the scope of this report, the Lawyers Committee notes its concern about this attitude. A government's willingness to allow independent human rights monitors to conduct investigations is an important index of its general human rights record. General Surin's position toward Amnesty International is particularly regrettable because the human rights organization has been engaged in a comprehensive investigation of human rights conditions in Cambodia, which is closed to independent human rights monitors. Because of this, access to recent arrivals from Cambodia's interior now living in Thailand is vital to Amnesty International's research efforts.

31. See *Bangkok World*, "Khmers in torture case resettled in Sweden" (January 13, 1987); *Bangkok Post*, "Torture claim Khmers go to Sweden" (January 14, 1987).

IV. VIOLENCE PERPETRATED BY CAMBODIANS

Cambodians living on the Thai-Cambodian border have been subject to violent attacks by other Cambodians, often in connection with smuggling or black-market activities. Gangs of armed Cambodians have terrorized Khao I Dang, Site Two and other camps in the past two years. Thai villages have been similarly victimized. Armed with automatic weapons (AK-47 and M-16 rifles) and rocket-propelled grenade guns, the bandits strike at night, in groups as large as 30.

Some are thought to be deserters from the KPNLF army, and others have been responsible for violent abuses while still in active service in KPNLF military forces. Though enhanced security measures brought the problem under control in Khao I Dang in April 1985, and in Site Two in October 1985, a spate of recent incidents has underscored the need for more concerted efforts to protect camp residents from the bandits.

Displaced Cambodians and Vietnamese have been even more vulnerable to attack by other Cambodians before they reach the United Nations-assisted camps in Thailand, as they make their way to those camps. Cambodians and Vietnamese fleeing their homelands have often been raped and robbed by KPNLF and Khmer Rouge troops shortly before they reach the Thai border. Girls as young as 11 years old have been repeatedly gang-raped by KPNLF troops in particular. Once intercepted by these troops, the victims have often been detained at KPNLF bases along the border, where they are held until ''ransoms'' are paid by relatives abroad or in Thailand.

In late November 1986, the Thai government and the KPNLF reportedly took several steps to end such abuses. Though it remains to be seen whether those measures will be sufficient, they signal a welcome recognition of the gravity of the problem and the need to address it.

A. Cambodian Bandits

Banditry along the Thai-Cambodian border is hardly a new phenomenon. Before the KPNLF was formed in 1979, some areas of the border were controlled by Cambodian "warlords," who had built up positions of power by controlling lucrative black markets and by commanding the loyalty of often brutal armed troops.[1] A number of these warlords became military commanders of the KPNLF, and, in the Front's early years, the areas they administered were characterized by frequent robberies, beatings, rapes and even murders.[2]

Though subsequent years saw improvements in the behavior of KPNLF troops toward civilians,[3] that progress was reversed during 1985 and early 1986. In that period, raids on border settlements intensified as KPNLF discipline unraveled in the wake of the devastating 1984-85 dry season offensive by Vietnamese troops. A large number of KPNLF troops deserted in the wake of that operation, and factional splits within the KPNLF in the past year have exacerbated problems of discipline among those who remained in the Front. In late 1985, long-simmering tensions within the KPNLF led to a division within its ranks. Many key military commanders and a number of civilian leaders formed a dissident faction, whose figurehead is KPNLF Commander-in-Chief Gen. Sak Sutsakhan. While opposing certain policies of Son Sann,[4] the dissidents still insist that

---

1. See Lawyers Committee for Human Rights, *Kampuchea: After the Worst* (August 1985) at 215.

2. *Id.*

3. KPNLF President Son Sann has frequently admonished his commanders to exert greater discipline with respect to abusive troops. See *id.* at 216-226.

4. The policy difference cited most frequently by the dissidents concerns cooperation between the KPNLF and the Sihanoukist forces. The dissidents oppose what they view as Son Sann's unwillingness to seek closer collaboration with the other non-communist guerrilla force. See, e.g., Paul Quinn-Judge, "Divided we shall fall," *Far Eastern Economic Review* (October 24, 1985). Son Sann, on the other hand, asserts that resistance to his efforts to impose greater discipline was a more decisive factor behind the split. Interview by Floyd Abrams and Diane Orentlicher with Son Sann (January 9, 1987).

they recognize him as President of the KPNLF. In any case, with loyalties among the military commanders divided, efforts by the KPNLF leadership to impose discipline have been highly problematic.

Additionally, while the KPNLF military could offer some measure of protection to civilians against its own deserters when the Front's camps were in Cambodia, its ability to do so has lessened since the camps were relocated in Thailand. Since then, the Front's troops have been segregated from the civilians living in Thailand to avoid provoking Vietnamese attacks against the latter.

1. Identity of the Bandits

Though it is widely believed that most so-called "bandit" raids in the past two years were carried out by deserters from the KPNLF, it appears that some may have involved current KPNLF soldiers, while others apparently have been undertaken by Cambodians who maintain active contact with the KPNLF. Indeed, some observers believe that it would be difficult for the gangs to operate for a prolonged period, as they do, without being in some sort of contact with the KPNLF military structure.

KPNLF President Son Sann has acknowledged that his troops have been undisciplined and have looted villages.[5] And leaders of the KPNLF faction opposed to Son Sann have likewise acknowledged, at least implicitly, that some KPNLF troops have plundered Site Two.[6]

---

5. Reuters dispatch (August 9, 1985).

6. As noted below, in January 1987 KPNLF Commander-in-Chief Gen. Sak Sutsakhan — a leader of the faction opposed to Son Sann — told the Lawyers Committee that he would soon implement stricter controls over visits by KPNLF troops to their relatives in Site Two. See Section A.3., *infra.* This measure, he explained, would enble the KPNLF to keep abusive troops out of Site Two.

51

Press accounts of bandit raids in previous years also suggest that persons responsible for those raids were affiliated with the KPNLF. A 1984 newspaper account of a gang's raids on Thai villages claimed that the group was based in the KPNLF camp Nong Samet, then located on the Cambodian side of the border.[7] Another article described a bandit raid by men dressed in green uniforms and army fatigues.[8] A third article reported that "Kampuchean soldiers" from "Nong Chang" (presumably referring to the KPNLF camp known as "Nong Chan") had raped two Thai girls.[9]

2. Trends in Incidence of Banditry

Violent bandit raids occurred at Site Two and other camps during much of 1985. Typical of these was a raid by more than 20 bandits on September 29, 1985. According to eyewitnesses, at approximately 1 a.m., the bandits stormed through several houses in Site Two South. One young woman, Om Phol, was shot in the shoulder. Four neighbors were injured, three requiring hospitalization, when a rocket-propelled grenade that a bandit had fired exploded just outside their hut. One of them, Nim Phan, was eight months pregnant, and was wounded in the abdomen. Though she gave birth two weeks later, the child was never fully conscious and died six days later. Scars on all four victims — Nim's was a four-

---

7. Bangkok *Thai Rat* in Thai (September 1, 1984) (as reported by JPRS).

8. Bangkok *Ban Muang* in Thai (September 12, 1984) (as reported by JPRS).

9. *Bangkok Daily News* in Thai (September 23, 1984) (as reported by JPRS). Indeed, it appears that many of the raids have been committed by soldiers from Chea Chhut's Nong Chan command. His units — many of which originally banded together several years ago primarily to turn a profit from smuggling and banditry — have long had a reputation for lack of discipline and even brutality. As the PAVN substantially sealed the border in the wake of its 1984-85 offensive, Chea Chhut's ability to pay and restrain his troops diminished as his profits from control over much of the once lucrative border trading dried up. Many then reverted to raiding Cambodian settlements and nearby Thai villages. As noted in section B, *infra*, Chea Chhut reportedly was removed as commander of Nong Chan in late November 1986 as part of a broader reform of KPNLF military practices.

inch wound — supported their accounts, which were also confirmed by medical records and by the doctor and refugee medical assistants who treated them.

Four days earlier, at about 12:30 a.m., some 20 robbers ravaged a different part of Site Two South, beating several residents and raiding at least nine homes in which some 50 people lived. They also forced the female residents to strip so that the bandits could probe their private parts for gold, a practice that appears to be common during such robberies. Sok Sovanarith, the chief of the *ilot* (subsection of the camp), was tied up and beaten unconscious as the brigands accused him of withholding information concerning the whereabouts of supposedly hidden gold. His assistant, Son Seth, also was severely beaten. Son's assailant was on the verge of stabbing him when another bandit pulled the knife-wielder away. One medical assistant who treated Sok said that his skull showed through the back of his head. Interviewing Sok one month after the injury occurred, the Lawyers Committee observed a prominent scar there.

Attacks by Cambodian bandits were also common at Khao I Dang during the early months of 1985. One that claimed several lives took place on March 10, 1985, when a band of robbers rampaged through Khao I Dang from 8 p.m. until 1 a.m. Sroy Khoeung, a resident of Khao I Dang, described to the Lawyers Committee how his wife, Sroy Chan, and an eight-month-old son, Khoeung Sooey, were shot and then blown up by a grenade which the robbers fired in their direction. A neighbor and her four-month-old daughter also were killed.[10] When the robbers attacked, Sroy Khoeung had fled his house, leaving his wife and child behind, believing that the robbers would harm only men. Having already been robbed three times, the family had nothing to give the bandits.

---

10. Sroy Khoeung's Food (identity) Card confirmed the deaths of his wife and son with red lines through their names and the notation "died, robbery victim, 10-3-85." All four deaths were reported in *The New York Times* on March 23, 1985. A very reliable written report indicated that a fifth victim was killed during the March 10 raid, and that six others were wounded.

A number of other raids plagued Khao I Dang in early 1985. They included a January 19 attack, during which a 14-year-old boy was shot dead and two women were raped. On January 25 bandits killed a man who had been accepted for resettlement in the United States. On February 25 a grenade killed a 16-month-old baby, wounded four other camp residents, and seriously wounded two Thai rangers. Four people were wounded on March 28. A rocket or grenade exploded less than 1,000 feet from the camp hospital on April 3, prompting the parents of many young patients to pull out their intravenous feeding tubes and flee the hospital with their children.

Several Cambodians told the Lawyers Committee that it is a common bandit practice to demand money or gold from camp residents, shouting "Can't you hear me?" and then slashing the victims' ears if there is no acceptable reply.

At the peak of the Khao I Dang violence, from January through March 1985, the gangs raided the camp on almost a weekly basis. Seeking safety far away from the camp fence, hundreds of residents flocked from their huts near the camp's perimeter to the hospital area and to other facilities every evening to sleep. When the safety of the hospital area itself became uncertain, many of them paid residents of Section Three, an area well inside Khao I Dang, for the use of their space. A western medical organization, Medicins Sans Frontieres (Doctors Without Borders), temporarily pulled its night team out of the camp on January 25 and again on March 12 because of the danger there.

The bandit raids abated at Khao I Dang in April 1985 due to improved security measures. These included the introduction there of additional Thai ranger guards, improved communications facilities among rangers, and nighttime lighting around the camp fence. Also, the UNHCR began to assign personnel to stay at Khao I Dang several nights each week, without announcing in advance which nights it would do so, as an additional security measure. Similarly, the belated transfer of a ranger unit to Site Two South around October 1985 helped minimize the gangs' attacks there. But, as one experienced relief worker observed, "Security waxes and wanes at the camps," and the situation at both Khao I Dang and Site Two deteriorated once again in 1986.

Although the banditry at Khao I Dang has never returned to pre-April 1985 levels, the Khao I Dang Annex was raided three times in February and March 1986. During the first of these intrusions, in early February, a few bandits armed with AK-47's severely fractured a middle-aged Cambodian woman's skull after she told them there were no young women in her hut, and roughed up several other Annex residents.

In a subsequent raid on March 5, about a dozen heavily armed bandits beat up several Annex residents and wounded a ranger. This incident reportedly marked the first time that bandits employed radios, apparently communicating with associates outside the camp fence and suggesting a measure of greater sophistication in their methods.

What may have been the same group returned on March 17, again using radios. They beat a number of Annex residents, and exchanged gunfire with Thai rangers. One ranger was killed and another was wounded. In the wake of this incident, Task Force 80 opened the gate between Khao I Dang and the Annex, allowing many Annex residents to sleep in the Khao I Dang hospital area for greater security.[11]

Since then, such violent bandit attacks have largely abated at Khao I Dang. In contrast, banditry remains a serious problem at Site Two, which was raided repeatedly during September and October 1986. Attacking on practically a weekly basis — and even more frequently in late October — the gangs apparently have felt confident enough on some occasions to take as long as 40 minutes to plunder the camp. Relief officials servicing the border camps told the Lawyers Committee in January 1987 that the problem of banditry at Site Two "is not getting any better."

---

11. As described in Chapter III, three Cambodian residents of Khao I Dang and the Annex who were thought to be involved in this incident were tortured by Task Force 80 officials several days later.

The bandits' attacks have taken a heavy toll. During a raid in mid-October 1986, one Vietnamese man was killed and three were wounded by bandit rifle fire. A Cambodian man also was shot and wounded later that same night, perhaps by the same band. A little more than a week later, five Cambodians were wounded — two of them seriously — by a bandit's exploding grenade during a robbery in Site Two South.

Thais living along the border have also been victimized by this recent banditry. An attack in early March 1986 was directed against the village of Kok Rakar, located about three miles from Site Two. A grenade, fired at a villager's home, wounded three and took the life of a 13-year-old Thai girl.

More recently, several months ago the vehicle of a private voluntary agency was attacked by robbers near Site Two. The attackers were believed to be Cambodians.

3. Recent Efforts to Address the Problem of Banditry

None of the KPNLF or Thai officials interviewed by the Lawyers Committee in January 1987 denied the truth of the foregoing allegations.[12] Instead, our discussions focused on measures planned or already taken to address the problem.

Representatives of the KPNLF faction that has challenged the leadership of Son Sann described several such measures.[13]

---

12. As previously noted, a draft of this report was furnished to Thai officials one month before our visit, and copies were made available to KPNLF leaders during our visit.

13. This faction's notable attention to these issues during our visit seems, at least in part, to reflect its relatively strong relationship with the Thai government. As a matter of official policy, the Thai government has taken the position that the split within the KPNLF is an internal matter which the two factions must resolve without outside interference. While it thus officially refuses to "take sides," in practice it is supportive of the dissident faction. This is reflected, for example, in the fact that it now channels materiel support to the KPNLF through dissident leader Gen. Sak instead of KPNLF President Son Sann.

Similarly, the Thai government has addressed its concerns about KPNLF abuses principally to Gen. Sak, imploring him to take measures to curb the abuses. See section B.3., *infra*. It has, in effect, designated him — rather than

One effort involved stricter control over the movement of KPNLF troops in and out of Site Two. Abdul Gaffar Peang Meth, a civilian leader of the dissident KPNLF faction, told us that KPNLF Commander-in-Chief Gen. Sak Sutsakhan had recently moved out of Site Two all civilian and military personnel who have "created unrest." Henceforth, both Dr. Gaffar and Gen. Sak told us, the KPNLF General Staff would more strictly control visits by soldiers to Site Two, where many of them have close relatives. In this way, soldiers known to have acted abusively in the past would be prevented from entering the camp.

Additionally, according to Dr. Gaffar, Gen. Sak had pledged that incidents of banditry by KPNLF soldiers or civilians would be severely punished. As noted below, an order dated January 1, 1987 establishing a committee that would investigate allegations of abuse by soldiers was prepared for Gen. Sak's signature,[14] while violations by civilians at Site Two would be investigated by the central civilian administration there.

Additionally, Dr. Gaffar announced, the KPNLF would consolidate the camps that now constitute Site Two into one centrally governed camp. This, he explained, would better enable the KPNLF to gain control over abusive elements within the camps.

Son Sann — as the KPNLF leader responsible for disciplining abusive troops and for taking other measures to prevent future abuses.

As a practical matter, Son Sann's ability to exert discipline over KPNLF troops may be more limited now than it has ever been. He told the Lawyers Committee in January 1987 that he was prevented by figures loyal to Gen. Sak from even visiting Site Two, the largest grouping of Cambodian civilians in Thailand. And while KPNLF commander Chea Chhut — whose troops have been linked most often to the so-called bandits — is thought to be loyal to Son Sann, Chea Chhut's ability to control his own troops appears to be lessening. In the two years since Chea Chhut's military base was overrun by Vietnamese forces, large numbers of his troops have "defected" to the command of Liv Ne, who is said to be loyal to Gen. Sak's faction.

14. See section B.3., *infra*.

Dr. Gaffar also announced that two battalions whose troops had committed robberies at Site Two, battalions 217 and 218, had been disbanded. When we asked Gen. Sak about this development, he explained that the commanders of the two battalions had been summoned to answer to him regarding the allegations of banditry. Instead of appearing, the two fled "into the interior [of Cambodia]," and their former troops were merged into other battalions.

For its part, the Thai government has decided to legalize market activity at Site Two. Since much of the banditry has been related to black market activity there, Thai officials hope to minimize the banditry by, in effect, removing the conditions that have helped foster it.

A recurring theme emerged in our discussions with Thai and KPNLF officials regarding efforts to control violence at Site Two. It concerns the important question of whose responsibility it is to control abuses there. In essence, the Thai government takes the position that the KPNLF's status at Site Two is that of a "government in exile," and that the Front therefore should assume primary responsibility for maintaining law and order there.

While this view stems from Thailand's broader effort to promote the guerrilla coalition as the legitimate government of Cambodia, it significantly affects the manner in which problems relating to the security of the civilians in Site Two are addressed. It means, for example, that the principal responsibility for disciplining Cambodian bandits lies with the civilian administration at Site Two. Thai and KPNLF officials also told us of plans to improve the security at Site Two by strengthening an existing system of joint patrols, with KPNLF forces taking primary responsibility for patrolling inside the camps, and Thai security personnel assuming principal responsibility for patrolling outside the camp perimeter.

The Lawyers Committee believes that Thailand must be prepared to assume responsibility for addressing security problems posed by Cambodian bandits when the Cambodian administration itself proves unable to provide adequate protection. Banditry proliferated, after all, under a system in which the Cambodians were, in principle, responsible for maintaining order within Site Two. And a number of Cambodians who hold responsible positions within the civilian administration at camps in Site Two have themselves been implicated in black market activities. While renewed efforts to strengthen discipline within the KPNLF surely deserve encouragement, it should be borne in mind that similar efforts in the past have encountered formidable resistance, even when the KPNLF administered zones in Cambodia itself — a situation theoretically more conducive to the success of such efforts.[15] Finally, the proliferation of banditry following the 1984/85 offensive by Vietnamese troops reflected the general unraveling of discipline within the KPNLF in the wake of that offensive, a development whose continuing effects are evident in such matters as the ongoing rift within the KPNLF. Against this background, we do not believe that the security of the Cambodians in Site Two would receive adequate protection if left to the charge of the Khmer administration there.

Accordingly, the Lawyers Committee believes that the Thai government must be prepared to assume ultimate responsibility for the protection of the displaced Cambodians as long as they remain in Thailand. Consistent with its desire to promote more effective governance within the Khmer administration at Site Two, Thailand should be prepared to exercise there its general responsibility for law enforcement with respect to criminal behavior occurring in Thai territory.

As a practical matter, the success of Thailand's efforts to promote a more effective law enforcement role by the Khmer administration at Site Two depends upon Thailand's active support in any case. The Khmer police patrols there are unarmed, and depend upon Task Force 80 to respond to actual incidents of banditry. We understand that the Khmer patrols now lack adequate communications devices for summoning Task Force 80 when an incident occurs. While Thai authorities indicated that this shortcoming will

---

15. See Lawyers Committee for Human Rights, *Kampuchea: After the Worst* (August 1985) at 237-250.

be addressed, the problem underscores the need for Thailand to remain actively engaged in the process of providing protection against banditry at Site Two and other camps.

B. Rapes, Robberies and Detentions Near Rithisen, Chamkar Ko and Nong Chan

Vietnamese and Cambodians fleeing their homelands frequently have been raped and robbed by KPNLF troops shortly before reaching the Thai border. Once at the border, many have been detained for weeks or months at the KPNLF's Rithisen, Chamkar Ko and Nong Chan camps,[16] part of the "hidden border" of military bases that also hold civilians, and to which the ICRC and other international organizations do not have access. Some of these detainees have been allowed to proceed to Site Two only after relatives abroad have sent ransom payments. Others have drawn upon their own resources to pay for their release. Still others have been allowed to proceed to the camp with the promise that they would raise the required funds once there — a promise the commanders involved in the extortion have had reason to believe they could enforce, since they exert substantial control over residents of Site Two.

Once ransoms have been paid or arranged, the detainees have been handed over to a Thai military border unit, Task Force 838. Task Force 838 in turn has contacted the International Committee of the Red Cross (ICRC), which has transported the new arrivals to Site Two.

The more fortunate detainees have been transferred to Site Two when the ICRC learned of their identities without having to pay or arrange ransom (though this has not necessarily ensured that they would not be pressured into payments once they reached Site Two).

---

16. "Nong Chan" is the name for both a civilian camp constituting part of Site Two and a separate, affiliated, military base.

Cambodian girl in Khmer Rouge camp at Khao Sarapee, Thailand. 1985. (AP)

Above: Cambodians fleeing into Thailand. 1983. (Al Santoli)
Below: Cambodians fleeing from Vietnamese shelling near Site 8. 1986. (AP)

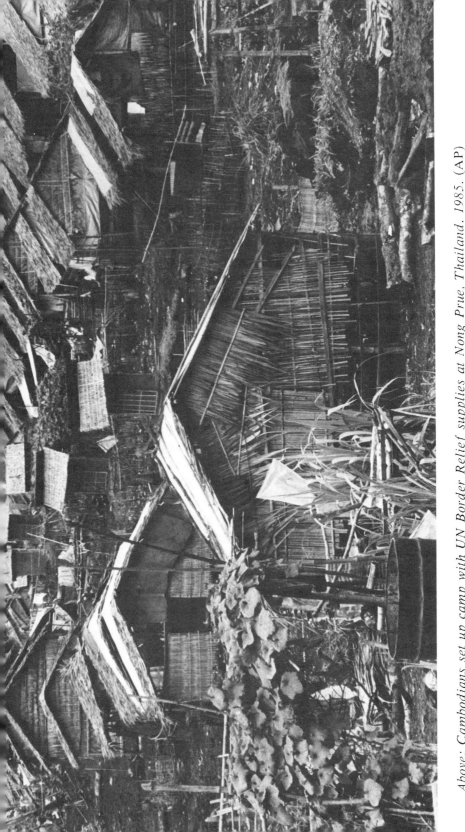

Above: Cambodians set up camp with UN Border Relief supplies at Nong Prue, Thailand. 1985. (AP)
Below: Thatch-and-bamboo huts at Site 2, where over 100,000 Cambodians reside. 1985. (Sharon May Brown)

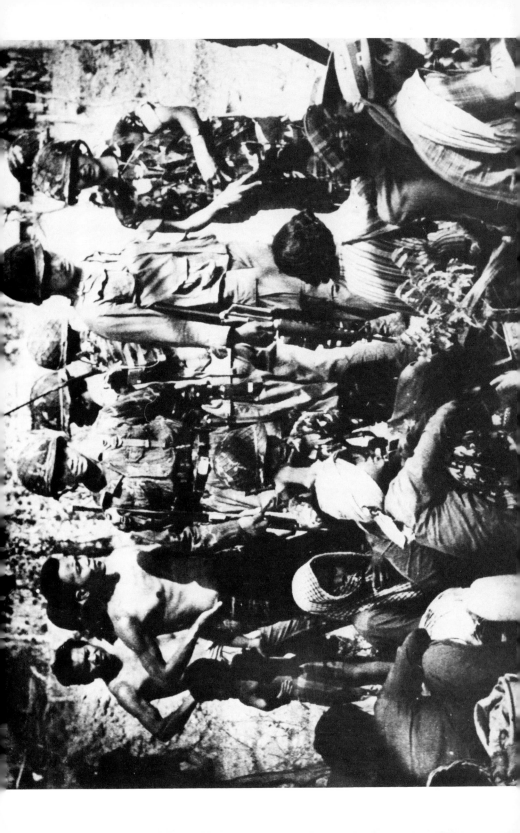

Above: Thai soldiers guarding Cambodians who have fled into Thailand. 1980. (AP)
Below: Cambodian children at Site 2. 1985. (Sharon May Brown)

Cambodian woman and child at Site 2. 1985. (Sharon May Brown)

Even when the ICRC has become aware of specific individuals' names, however, securing their release has sometimes required as many as ten ICRC entreaties to both local Thai and KPNLF military authorities.

At the end of November 1986, the Thai government, encouraged by representatives of the U.S. government, took steps to address these abuses. In response, the KPNLF claims to have taken action to end the abuses. It remains to be seen whether those steps, described below, will prove sufficient. Nevertheless, they signal a welcome indication that at least some of the responsible authorities are seeking to end the abuses.

1. Rithisen and Chamkar Ko

While much of the central border zone has been mined and fortified by the Vietnamese army, the vicinity of Rithisen — the military base corresponding to the civilian settlement known as Nong Samet — and Chamkar Ko has remained under the control of KPNLF commander Liv Ne, at least until November 1986. Most Vietnamese and Cambodians seeking to enter Thailand in the past year or more have passed through that area. Liv Ne's troops apparently have been responsible for most of the rapes and robberies (and all of the detentions), but there also have been reports of abuses by Cambodian bandits and Khmer Rouge soldiers. (The Khmer Rouge also maintain a sporadic presence near Rithisen, but usually operate deeper inside Cambodia.)

Both Cambodians and foreign observers interviewed by the Lawyers Committee assert that Vietnamese have suffered the most on the way to the border. Cambodians, particularly light-skinned women, also have been raped and robbed.

Typical of such abuse was the experience of two sisters, Thith Sarim (P), and Thith Teang (P), who were stopped just before they reached Thailand by six KPNLF soldiers, and were repeatedly raped by four of them. The sisters had been guided almost to the border by persons whom they had engaged in Phnom Penh, but the guides left them shortly before they encountered the soldiers.

Once at Chamkar Ko, the two were detained for approximately 33 days before ICRC workers took them to Site Two. They were not raped at Chamkar Ko, though the older sister had heard that other women were molested there. A Cambodian military commander instructed the two sisters to write to an aunt in the United States, asking for $3,000 to pay for their release. They complied. The sisters reported that the return address for the letter specified an officer's name, but they were unable to remember (or perhaps were afraid to state) his name or address.[17]

Another woman, Duong Pat (P), recounted a series of harrowing encounters as she made her way to Thailand. Duong, whose husband is in the United States, began her journey to the border in June 1985, and was accompanied by her father, father-in-law, brother-in-law and child. They were stopped by soldiers four times before reaching Rithisen. She identified the first three groups as KPNLF soldiers, and the last as Khmer Rouge. The motive each time was robbery, though the first group (of seven soldiers) left little for the subsequent thieves. During the first encounter, all seven soldiers raped Duong Pat, who was raped again by the leader of the Khmer Rouge group.

Duong Pat and her family arrived at Chamkar Ko in July 1985. She was immediately taken to Rithisen, and her family followed the next day. They remained there from July until October. Soon after she arrived at Rithisen, a commander forced Duong Pat to live with him. (The relatives lived in a separate location.) She and her relatives did not have to pay any ransom in order to leave Rithisen. Instead, they came to Site Two as part of a large relocation of soldiers' families and other persons.

---

17. The Lawyers Committee interviewed the sisters separately. Their versions of their rapes and detention were consistent, though their estimates of the duration of their detentions by the band of soldiers and then at Chamkar Ko each varied by a couple of days. In addition, the younger sister reported being struck by at least one soldier who raped her.

Over the course of three days before arriving at Chamkar Ko, Hong Sameth (P) and her 13-year-old daughter were raped several times, on one occasion by at least ten KPNLF soldiers. Hong's other daughter, who was eight years old, was not raped. Before the rapes, however, the soldiers probed the private parts of all three for gold. Arriving at Chamkar Ko on June 15, 1985, Hong was instructed to write to relatives in the United States requesting them to send a "ransom" in the sum of $1,500 per head. Nine days later, however, she was allowed to leave with several other persons whom the ICRC took to Site Two. She believes that her release may have been inadvertent, though it is possible that the ICRC secured her release. Hong and her daughters were not molested at Chamkar Ko.[18]

Chau Oeur (P), a man of 50, said that KPNLF soldiers robbed the group of relatives with which he was traveling and raped its women and teen-aged girls on July 30, 1985. He also said that the soldiers took away all 11 of these relatives, and that he has not seen them since.

Reports of similar abuse by Khmer Rouge troops are far less frequent. In recent months, however, there have been increasing reports of rapes and robberies by Khmer Rouge troops of fleeing Cambodians and Vietnamese before they reach the KPNLF-controlled area near Rithisen.

2. Nong Chan

A similar pattern of rape and extortion has been characteristic of the troops who, at least until recently, operated under the command of Chea Chhut. Once intercepted by those troops, the victims have been taken to the military base known as Nong Chan for detention.

---

18. The mother and older daughter were interviewed separately, and provided consistent accounts.

Again, Vietnamese females — even young girls — have borne the brunt of the abuse. In July of 1986, for example, as many as ten soldiers molested an 11 year-old Vietnamese girl whom they encountered outside of the Nong Chan military camp. Once inside the camp, the girl was not again sexually abused. After their release from Nong Chan, several other detainees provided foreign officials with consistent and detailed accounts documenting the regular rape of virtually all of the other females imprisoned there.

The ICRC obtained the freedom of the 11 year-old, two relatives aged 14 and 16, and four others only after repeatedly petitioning Thai and KPNLF authorities with a list of the seven individuals' names. It became aware of the girl's imprisonment after her relatives in the United States received letters seeking a ransom for the three children. The ICRC subsequently learned that at least another 20 persons remained imprisoned at Nong Chan.

3. Recent Efforts to Address Abuses

By late November 1986, the Thai government acted to put a stop to these abuses. In part because the extortion practices touched the lives of numerous Cambodians living in the United States — recipients of "ransom letters" from relatives detained on the Thai-Cambodian border — pressure had mounted within the United States to address the abuses.[19] Two officials of the Reagan Administration who visited Thailand in November 1986 expressed their concern about these abuses to Thai officials, who responded immediately. In late November, Gen. Wanchai Ruangtrakal, the Chief of Staff of the Royal Thai Army, met with a group of KPNLF military leaders.[20] Gen. Wanchai reportedly made it clear to the

---

19. Particularly important in this regard was the gathering and dissemination of confidential reports about abuses at Chamkar Ko, Rithisen and Nong Chan by Al Santoli, a U.S. journalist. His reports were distributed, on a confidential basis, to officials in the Reagan Administration, the Thai government and the KPNLF, and helped focus the attention of those officials on the problems at the border.

20. Both Liv Ne and Chea Chhut, commanders of the troops associated with most of the abuses, reportedly were present at the meeting.

KPNLF members present that the extortion and rape must stop immediately. In response, KPNLF Commander-in-Chief Gen. Sak Sutsakhan reportedly told Gen. Wanchai that the former had recently instituted severe punishment of KPNLF personnel who have committed the aforementioned abuses.

By that time, the ICRC and UNBRO had already taken action to remove the conditions in which the abuses had thrived. On October 25, 1986, the two organizations evacuated 1,187 civilians from Chamkar Ko, Rithisen and Nong Chan to Site Two, and still others were subsequently transferred.[21]

At the same time, the KPNLF claims to have transferred hundreds of military personnel from those three camps to a military outpost, described by one KPNLF figure as a "secret sanctuary" on the border. At that outpost, he explained, military leaders who commanded such bases as Nong Chan and Rithisen were being retrained and resupplied, and would thenceforth command troops that would be deployed in the Cambodian interior, and no longer would be "base commanders" operating on the border. While this development was adopted, we were told, to enhance the KPNLF's effectiveness as an armed opposition force, it would also serve, in effect, to "purge" the border area of corrupt practices. Included in the group thus re-assigned, the Lawyers Committee was told, were Liv Ne and Chea Chhut.[22] Only 100 troops per passageway were left to guard the entry points to Thailand on the border.[23]

---

21. This move served two objectives. First, it removed the civilians from the corrupt and abusive practices that proliferated at the three border camps. Second, it enforced the policy observed by Thailand, the KPNLF and the international relief organizations of separating civilians from military personnel, thereby removing a justification for Vietnamese forces to attack civilians.

22. Earlier reports had indicated that the two were dismissed from their commands.

23. Interview by Floyd Abrams and Diane Orentlicher with Abdul Gaffar Peang Meth (January 8, 1987).

In addition to this measure, Abdul Gaffar Peang Meth — a civilian leader of the dissident faction within the KPNLF — announced at a briefing arranged for the Lawyers Committee that Gen. Sak had appointed a committee to investigate reports of abuses by KPNLF troops. The order establishing the tribunal, which was made available to the Lawyers Committee, was dated January 1, 1987 and had not yet been signed by Gen. Sak.[24] Dr. Gaffar also announced that the KPNLF would establish a military court that would prosecute abusive soldiers on the basis of recommendations by the investigating committee. In a separate meeting with Gen. Sak, the Lawyers Committee was told that Liv Ne and Chea Chhut would be among the first to be investigated once the investigating committee began operating.[25]

As with other recent reforms announced during the Lawyers Committee's recent visit to Thailand, it is too soon to measure the efficacy of these actions. Clearly, concerted monitoring will be necessary to ensure their success.[26] And just as clearly, the very fact that the need to address the abuses has been recognized is a promising and potentially important development.

C. Vietnamese in Site Two

Vietnamese "land people" — displaced persons who made their way to Thailand by crossing through Cambodia rather than

---

24. Gen. Sak later told us that — the rift within the KPNLF notwithstanding — he still recognized Son Sann as the Front's President, and therefore would consult with him regarding the order before promulgating it. Interview by Floyd Abrams and Diane Orentlicher with Gen. Sak Sutsakhan (January 8, 1987).

25. *Id.* The Committee was able to interview Liv Ne regarding the allegations that his troops had committed rapes and had detained people for ransom at border entry points. He did not deny the basic allegations. Instead, he insisted that he had summoned his commanders, and was determined to "get to the bottom of this" and find out who was responsible for the abuses. Interview by Diane Orentlicher with Liv Ne (January 8, 1987).

26. For discussion of the role of the international relief community in this effort, see Chapter VIII.B., *infra.*

traveling by sea — remain especially vulnerable once they arrive in Thailand. Some 3,000 of these people are crowded into a camp within Site Two South, and thus are surrounded by a largely hostile population — Cambodians who oppose the Vietnamese occupation of their country.[27]

Such general hostility has given rise to overt violence at times of particular tension, such as when camps are threatened by Vietnamese shelling. In 1985, Cambodian medical assistants raped a Vietnamese woman visiting her sister in the Dong Ruk camp hospital within Site Two. On October 18, 1985, a grenade was tossed into the Vietnamese camp, killing two and injuring 15 others.[28] In mid-January 1985, when the Vietnamese were situated at Dong Ruk's original location inside Cambodia, as many as 20 Vietnamese women were raped by KPNLF soldiers who pillaged their section of the camp.[29] (Dong Ruk subsequently became part of Site Two.)

Several violent incidents have stemmed from Cambodian-Vietnamese business transactions that went sour. Apparently acting at the instigation of Task Force 80 soldiers, a small group of deserters from the Vietnamese army living in Site Two helped break up Cambodian market activity in the camp for a time. They reportedly also spied for the rangers, advising them which Cambodian homes might be worth robbing.

Violence directed at the Vietnamese in Site Two was alleviated, at least temporarily, by two developments in early 1986. First, Thailand has permitted the consideration of the Vietnamese for resettlement in the United States and other countries. Roughly

---

27. Historic ethnic — as well as political — tensions between Cambodians and Vietnamese cause many Cambodians in Thailand to resent even those Vietnamese who have fled their homeland and oppose their government's policies.

28. It is not clear, however, that the grenade incident stemmed from ethnic tensions.

29. In the face of a rapidly mounting dry season offensive by Vietnamese troops, the KPNLF guerrillas had retreated to Dong Ruk from other sites along the border. Thai military officers later confirmed that the rapes and robberies had occurred. See *Bangkok Post* (February 4, 1985).

1,700 have been accepted, leaving the remaining population at 3,000 or more (including recent arrivals).

Second, those who remain were moved from Site Two North to a more spacious area adjoining Site Two South (Nong Samet) in early 1986. Though UNBRO undertook this shift for health reasons — the new location is less cramped and offers better sanitation — a by-product is that the Site Two South Cambodian civilian administration may be better able to protect the Vietnamese from the surrounding population.

Nevertheless, the ability of the civilian administration to shield the Vietnamese is limited, at best. Even in Site Two South, the population remains exceedingly vulnerable.

V. DEMOCRATIC KAMPUCHEA (KHMER ROUGE) CONTROL OF CIVILIANS

The presence in Thailand of civilian encampments controlled by the guerrilla forces of Democratic Kampuchea (DK), commonly known as the Khmer Rouge, raises a special concern: the inability of those camps' residents to move to settlements affiliated with other opposition groups. In the wake of the 1984/85 Vietnamese offensive, some 59,000 Cambodians living under DK control have found shelter in Thailand, many in the border settlement known as Site Eight.[1] By common estimates, at least one-third of Site Eight's 30,000 residents would opt to move to one of the non-communist Cambodian settlements if given the choice. Officials of both the KPNLF and FUNCINPEC indicated in interviews with the Lawyers Committee that they would accept people from DK camps.

Asylum seekers typically have no claim to determine where, in a host country, they will live. But the exceptionally appalling human rights record of the Khmer Rouge should justify an exception in this case. At least one million Cambodians died during the era of DK rule, some from savage torture, others by summary execution, and still others from being literally worked or starved to death.

Operating as a guerrilla force since their regime was overthrown by the December 1978 Vietnamese invasion, the Khmer Rouge have exerted a high degree of social control over those whom they govern, despite a veneer of relative moderation.[2] The rigidity and brutality of Khmer Rouge rule have, however, been moderated somewhat since their camps were relocated on Thai soil. At least in Site Eight, armed guerrillas are no longer regularly available to enforce civilian administration edicts. The international relief agencies that assist the camp residents — barred from having contact

---

1. The rest live in four other border camps: Ta Luan, Borai, Samrong Kiat, and Natrao.

2. For detailed discussion of DK human rights practices since 1979, see Lawyers Committee for Human Rights, *Kampuchea: After the Worst* (August 1985).

with the civilian residents when the camps were located in Cambodia — also seem to have had an ameliorating influence on the behavior of camp authorities. During the Lawyers Committee's October 1985 visit, this liberalization was evidenced by a wedding celebration, flourishing market activity, and, most significantly, the willingness of Site Eight residents to discuss conditions in the camp.[3]

Rigid control nonetheless remains a feature of life in the Khmer Rouge camps. Most persons interviewed, for example, reported that the camp administration issued injunctions against the residents' approaching the ICRC or other foreigners with complaints or requests for transfer to non-communist camps. And, while armed guerrillas are not permitted to live inside Site Eight, these and other injunctions are enforced with the help of DK cadres and informants who abound there.

Many camp residents speak with foreigners in obvious fear of such informants. One interview at Sight Eight was conducted in hushed tones, with someone standing watch outside. To avoid detection at the conversation's conclusion, the Lawyers Committee's delegate, Stephen Golub, was asked to leave the hut where the interview was conducted only when an ''all clear'' signal was given, and to walk to the camp's nearest main road by an indirect route. Another interview, with a palpably terrified subject, was prematurely terminated when a uniformed man hovered outside the room.[4]

---

3. These conditions stood in striking contrast to those that a previous Lawyers Committee delegation observed when they visited DK settlements inside Cambodia in November 1984.

4. Partly because of the difficulty of arranging interviews which the Lawyers Committee delegate felt would not endanger the Site Eight residents involved, those discussions were supplemented by interviews with members of two small groups of civilians who, shortly before Mr. Golub visited Thailand, had been allowed to leave Site Eight to rejoin family members in Site Two's San Ro camp.

A. Removal to Phnom Dey

What these Cambodians fear, above all, is forced removal to Phnom Dey, a Khmer Rouge logistics base that constitutes part of the "hidden border" in Thailand.[5]

1. Removal for Detention

According to several civilians, a number of individuals had been forcibly removed because they had broken the Khmer Rouge rule against telling "barang" (Caucasians) about their discontent or desire to move to a non-communist camp. These individuals reportedly were taken to Phnom Dey for "re-education."

One such person was an interpreter/leader named Mr. Heung. Though not every source interviewed about Mr. Heung could recall exactly when he left, one woman who was interviewed in Site Two believed that he was taken to Phnom Dey in May 1985 because he was a leader of people who wanted to leave Site Eight for a non-communist camp. A relief worker confirmed being approached by Mr. Heung regarding his desire to transfer to a non-communist camp shortly before he disappeared. The woman in Site Two named seven other alleged leaders who were trucked off to Phnom Dey at night along with Heung, including two whom other Cambodians identified as having been taken there. These eight apparently were part of a group of between 100 and 200 civilians whom a foreign correspondent reported were forcibly removed from May 17 to May 21.[6] Three Cambodians interviewed by the Lawyers Committee added that the prisoners' families also were taken to Phnom Dey soon afterwards.

---

5. Phnom Dey is also known by the designation "Site Eight North." Informed observers believe that additional DK-controlled civilians may be at another DK logistics base in Thailand known as "Site Eight West."

6. Paul Quinn-Judge, "Knowing thy enemy," *Far Eastern Economic Review* (June 6, 1985) at 16.

What happens after individuals are taken to Phnom Dey for re-education is not certain, but is indicated by recent testimony and previous DK policy. Re-education is punishment; some Cambodians interviewed used the terms interchangeably. In a November 1984 interview with Lawyers Committee representatives visiting Khmer Rouge camps that were then in Cambodia, DK leader Ieng Sary acknowledged that certain behavior could lead to detention, in places he referred to as "instruction halls."[7] In October 1985, the Lawyers Committee interviewed three of at least 32 women and children who had been placed in an "instruction hall" after an unsuccessful attempt to escape the DK's Klong Wa camp in October 1984. They referred to the facilities as "Ta Seum's Place" or "Prison 80," a jail for those committing medium-level offenses.

Their accounts of conditions in Ta Seum's Place were consistent with each other and with those previously provided by other prisoners:[8] They received meager rations of rice, and worked two shifts a day (with a break in between) making punji stakes[9] and carrying out other tasks related to military purposes. They were not physically abused, but were housed near a group of about a dozen men whose hands and feet were manacled. They were evacuated to Site Eight when Vietnamese troops started shelling the surrounding area. Once there, the former prisoners were treated like other camp residents. They were not again imprisoned, but were repeatedly warned not to make contact with the ICRC.

2. Removal for Conscription as Military Porters

Some civilians have been forcibly removed to Phnom Dey to work as military porters. Several Cambodians and other sources

---

7. See Lawyers Committee for Human Rights, *Kampuchea: After the Worst* (August 1985) at 191.

8. Conditions at Ta Seum's Place are described in Lawyers Committee for Human Rights, *Kampuchea: After the Worst* (August 1985) at 187-199.

9. Punji stakes are bamboo spears embedded upright in hidden holes. They are designed to impale unsuspecting enemy troops.

reported that the camp administration periodically pressures residents to go to Phnom Dey to help transport supplies. One said that she had witnessed a group of ten men being taken away at gunpoint, with their hands tied behind their backs, for this purpose one night in September 1985.[10] One of the men in this group, a neighbor named Moeun, previously had refused to carry guns and supplies to the Cambodian interior. The witness added that she had been threatened with similar conscription or imprisonment after refusing repeated requests to serve in this manner. Her claim is buttressed by the aforementioned press account of the May 1985 forcible relocation of 100-200 Cambodians from Site Eight: a Khmer Rouge cadre reportedly explained to camp residents that some of those (involuntarily) removed were to work as porters.[11]

Even when efforts to press civilians into transport service are not backed by arms, they instill palpable fear among those who would resist. One person interviewed by the Lawyers Committee was so frightened after turning down a request that he perform military transport services that he slept in a friend's hut at night rather than his own. After more than ten years of Khmer Rouge domination and indoctrination, many other camp residents would not think to question their leaders' orders. Not seeing any alternatives, some might accept assurances that the treatment or discipline in store for them would be light. For example, on the night a Mr. Teum was permanently removed from Site Eight, he told one person (whom the Lawyers Committee subsequently interviewed) that he was going "to study" for just one week. But the bottom line was best expressed by a relief worker: "A lot of these people are so scared, they won't refuse to go."

Relocation to Phnom Dey can mean a fate worse than imprisonment. Persons transporting supplies to DK guerrillas inside the

---

10. Other information provided by this woman was confirmed by an informed foreign observer.

11. Paul Quinn-Judge, "Knowing thy enemy," *Far Eastern Economic Review* (June 6, 1985) at 16. The article also suggested that some persons who were taken to Phnom Dey were soldiers and medical orderlies.

Cambodian interior enter a war zone. They may be captured by Vietnamese or PRK forces, or fall victim to the crossfire of battle or the mine-strewn border.[12] Though DK reliance on these "military porters" reportedly has diminished as it has rebuilt its influence inside Cambodia, many civilians still run the risk of transport duty.

3. Mass Relocations

Not all DK transfers of Site Eight residents to Phnom Dey are individually targeted or the result of overtly coerced relocation. Starting in early August 1985, over 5,000[13] civilians were trucked to Phnom Dey and possibly to other locations under the cover of night. The rate of the transfers progressively increased until Thai authorities brought them to a halt in September 1985. Most of those transferred reportedly were relatives of soldiers, and presumably went willingly. But the ten previously-noted men who were taken out at gunpoint would have been included in this group, and implicit coercion backs virtually any significant instruction by Khmer Rouge camp administrators.

---

12. Though an estimate that the Vietnamese have laced the border with more than one million mines ("Vietnam thinks again," *The Economist* (May 24, 1986) at 44) seems excessive, there is no doubt that thousands of mines have been planted to counter guerrilla infiltration.

13. The precise figure is unknown, though it almost certainly ranged into the thousands. The estimate of over 5,000 removed from Site Eight stems from the difference between a "headcount" which UNBRO conducted at the camp on March 3, 1985 and one it conducted on November 2, 1985. The actual UNBRO count at any border camp it services is of females over 1.1 meters tall (i.e., presumably over 10 years old). This number is then multiplied by a predetermined factor to estimate a camp's total population, or "headcount," of food distribution beneficiaries. Because of the extraordinarily high birth rate in the border camps, UNBRO raised this multiplication factor from 2.5 for the March 3 count to 2.75 for the one conducted on November 2. While the resulting population totals for almost all of the other border camps rose accordingly, that of Site Eight dropped by more than 2,000. It presumably would have risen, instead, by well over 3,000, had the Khmer Rouge not removed civilians from the camp. Informed observers confirmed that thousands were taken out of Site Eight.

The mass transfers seemed designed to implement the desire of some DK leaders to relocate all of Site Eight. From time to time they have pressed Thai authorities to move the camp to a more isolated spot even closer to the border, where the "corrupting" influence of foreign relief organizations might be restricted or eliminated — in effect, to make all 30,000 Site Eight residents part of the hidden border. The mass transfers of August-September 1985 accomplished precisely that end; UNBRO does not supply Phnom Dey,[14] and the ICRC does not have access to it.

Several well-informed sources strongly suspect that some elements of the DK leadership have orchestrated a number of violent incidents to persuade the Thai government that Site Eight's population is in danger and therefore should be moved to Phnom Dey or to another location (which presumably would be inaccessible to foreign observers). Each incident forced a partial or total temporary evacuation. On May 14, 1985, 30 to 40 Khmer Rouge soldiers ran through the camp shouting, shooting their guns in the air and firing rocket-propelled grenades. At least one civilian was killed and several others were injured that night. On separate occasions shortly after that, unidentified armed elements believed to be DK soldiers engaged Thai forces in a firefight behind the camp, and in broad daylight four or five shells fell very close to it. According to one eyewitness, during an October 23, 1985 disturbance, DK soldiers again ran through the camp shooting, and shouting, "Go to Phnom Dey!"

More recently, on May 29, 1986, a series of shells fell into the middle of Site Eight.[15] Though Thai officials blame Vietnamese troops for the barrage, a number of observers suspect that DK troops were responsible; the attack occurred on the very day that some civilians living in a military DK camp were to be transferred

---

14. UNBRO ceased supplying Phnom Dey earlier in 1985, because Thai authorities had posed an unusual requirement that UNBRO provide 24 to 48 hours' advance notice of any food deliveries to the camp, and because of its military nature.

15. See Chapter VI, *infra*.

to Site Eight — a move the Khmer Rouge reportedly opposed. At least 11 camp residents were killed by the shelling;[16] two were children. An observer who visited the camp shortly afterwards was told that the other persons killed in the incident were women and the elderly. Between 30 and 50 Cambodians, mostly children, were injured by the blasts.[17]

The Khmer Rouge reluctance to permit foreign access to Site Eight is mirrored in the other camps it controls. In fact, a February 1986 UNBRO report noted that in three of the other four DK border settlement areas — Ta Luan, Borai and Samrong Kiat — the camp administrators were resisting UNBRO's attempts to maintain appropriate access, despite the fact that this could force UNBRO to cut off relief aid to those settlements.[18] Another UNBRO report published several months later extended this concern to Natrao, the only other DK-controlled camp, as well.[19] Since being driven across the border into Thailand, then, it seems that the Khmer Rouge leadership has consistently tried to deny or restrict the contact between civilians under its control and foreign relief organizations.

B. Relocation to Cambodia

It appears that some of the Cambodians relocated to Phnom Dey were transferred from there to Cambodia. Still others have been removed directly from DK camps in Thailand to Cambodia.

According to informed sources, in March 1986 approximately 1,500 residents of the DK's Samrong Kiat camp returned to

---

16. Address by Khachadpai Burusapatana, Deputy Secretary General of Thailand's National Security Council, at a UNHCR meeting in Geneva (October 7, 1986), as reported in *Bangkok Post* (October 8, 1986).

17. *Refugee Reports*, Vol. VII, No. 6 (June 13, 1986) at 7.

18. United Nations Border Relief Operation, *Situation Report as at February 15, 1986* at 2.

19. United Nations Border Relief Operation, *Situation Report as at June 9, 1986* at 1.

Cambodia from the northern part of the border. While there is no direct evidence that they did not go back "voluntarily," it is noteworthy that a news article previously reported that some residents of Samrong Kiat want to leave, preferring to live under the control of Prince Sihanouk's FUNCINPEC.[20] A substantial part of the 5,000 or more civilians moved from Site Eight to Phnom Dey in August and September of 1985 might have ended up back inside Cambodia, at a DK military base.[21]

The possibility of mass transfers of civilians by DK leaders back into Cambodia is consistent with evidence that the number of civilians living in DK border camps has diminished substantially since 1983. UNBRO headcounts indicate that the population of the Ta Luan camp dropped from 8,790 on January 24, 1983 to 3,872 on November 11, 1985.[22] To be sure, these figures must be evaluated with caution: the difficulties inherent in conducting headcounts back in 1983 may make the resulting totals inaccurate. And, as previously noted, the hidden border could well have absorbed a chunk of any "missing" population.

Nevertheless, the recent removal of 1,500 persons from Samrong Kiat to Cambodia suggests the possibility that others may have been taken into the Cambodian interior before — and that more may follow. The voluntariness and extent of these removals may never become known.

C. Current Khmer Rouge Leadership

Beyond specific allegations of mistreatment, the very identity of Khmer Rouge authorities lends a humanitarian urgency to the desire of those who seek to leave their control. The unparalleled brutality

---

20. Paul Quinn-Judge, "The super-camp risk," *Far Eastern Economic Review* (September 5, 1985) at 17.

21. See *id*.

22. United Nations Border Relief Operation tables detailing Beneficiaries of Food Distribution for Khmer Civilians as of May 27, 1985 (for the January 1, 1983 headcount) and as of January 6, 1986 (for the November 16, 1985 headcount).

of the Khmer Rouge when they ruled Cambodia in the late 1970's is, of course, well known. The same leadership that presided over the mass murders of that era remain substantially in control today. They include Ieng Sary, formerly Chairman of the State Presidium and now a Minister in the CGDK cabinet, and Khieu Samphan, formerly Deputy Premier of Democratic Kampuchea and now the Vice Chairman of the State of Democratic Kampuchea in charge of Foreign Affairs.

Notwithstanding Pol Pot's widely-publicized "retirement" as the DK's top military commander, it is widely believed that the announcement was little more than a public-relations device, with Pol Pot still calling the shots, at least until his recent reported illness. Other key figures in the DK leadership remain in important positions. Pol Pot's official successor, Son Sen, was the DK central committee member to whom the director of the S.21 (Tuol Sleng) extermination center in Phnom Penh directly reported while supervising the torture and execution of 20,000 persons from 1975 to 1978.[23] Kong Kech Eav and Tong Sin Hean, respectively the extermination center's director and chief of interrogation, also retain positions of authority in the Khmer Rouge structure.[24]

Ny Kan, who now commands the DK military's 320th Division and has substantial authority over Site Eight and Phnom Dey, was a ranking Foreign Ministry official when the Pol Pot regime was in power. He also has been implicated in the December 1978 murder of a visiting British academic in Phnom Penh.[25] Similarly, informed observers report that Ta Mok, notorious for his supervision of a sweeping series of purges and massacres throughout much of Cambodia when the Khmer Rouge ruled the country, wields control over the northern DK border camp of Natrao and over at least part of the Samrong Kiat camp's population. He also remains a top official

---

23. David Hawk, "Tuol Sleng extermination centre," *Index on Censorship* (January 1986) at 31.

24. See *id*.

25. Paul Quinn-Judge, "Knowing thy enemy," *Far Eastern Economic Review* (June 6, 1985) at 16.

within the DK's command structure.

The continued domination of part of the border population by those who bear ultimate responsibility for the deaths of at least one in seven Cambodians is cause enough for concern about how the Khmer Rouge treat civilians whom they control, particularly those who remain under DK control involuntarily. These concerns are magnified when the Cambodians are placed beyond the protective reach of international observation at Phnom Dey and inside Cambodia. The history of Khmer Rouge atrocities is a spectre stalking those Cambodians' future.

D. Thai Policies Regarding Khmer Rouge Camps

1. Khmer Rouge Control Over Civilians

With some notable exceptions, Thai policies generally have tolerated and even enforced Khmer Rouge control over displaced Cambodians. This pattern of cooperation reaches back to shortly after the Vietnamese invasion deposed the Pol Pot regime. Thai authorities allowed the Khmer Rouge to exert virtually complete control over Khao Laan, the first camp established in Thailand for displaced Cambodians. After establishing and assigning persons under DK control to a second camp, the Sakeo I Holding Center, in October 1979, Thai authorities permitted DK cadres to hold sway over food distribution, as well as other aspects of daily life in the camp. The Royal Thai Government has permitted the Khmer Rouge to maintain its grip on a segment of the border population in the succeeding years.

On two occasions in recent years, however, Thai authorities allowed civilians living under DK control to defect to KPNLF camps. The first occurred on May 24, 1983, when UNBRO and the ICRC coordinated a surprise move in which civilians in Red Hill, a temporary DK evacuation site, were offered the choice of going to KPNLF camps or departing for DK camps. Some 2,700 persons opted to move to KPNLF-affiliated camps. Although the move was coordinated by UNBRO and the ICRC, it could not have been implemented without at least tacit Thai approval. But on that same day at Red Hill, armed DK troops herded other civilians onto buses going to the DK camps while outnumbered Thai soldiers simply looked on.

The strains in Thai policy, and quite possibly in the Thai military as well, again arose in October 1984. At that time, 582 persons escaped from the DK's Klong Wa camp inside Cambodia, and were allowed to proceed to the KPNLF's San Ro camp. Yet just a week later, a group of 50 attempting a similar escape from Klong Wa to San Ro was intercepted by Thai soldiers and taken to O'Sralou, another DK camp. While the reasons for such unofficial policy moves cannot be known, some informed observers believe that Thai authorities, fearing that a wave of escapes that would divest the DK of its civilian base (and thus any remaining shreds of legitimacy), decided to discourage future attempts.[26] It is possible that the second group was taken to O'Sralou, and not back to Klong Wa, because the O'Sralou administration was reportedly less repressive, and therefore likely to treat the would-be defectors more leniently.

Now that the DK camps are in Thailand, the Royal Thai Government's policy of generally cooperating with the Khmer Rouge retains threads of ambivalence. Informed observers report that the government has resisted DK pressure to move Site Eight. As noted above, it eventually halted the massive August-September 1985 relocations from Site Eight to Phnom Dey by barring or restricting the DK practice of trucking out civilians at night. And restricting or eliminating the DK military's access to Site Eight has improved the civilians' welfare considerably.

But in other respects the Khmer Rouge are still left to do what they please. Thai authorities generally decline to intercept or interfere with punitive removals to Phnom Dey, where the ICRC is

---

26. At the time of a Lawyers Committee delegation's visit to the border shortly after these incidents, it was thought by a number of people in the relief community that the payment of bribes may have been a decisive factor. According to these sources, Thai authorities typically returned to DK authorities, upon payment of a "ransom," civilians who tried to escape DK control and were intercepted by Thai authorities. It was believed that the group that escaped in October 1984 was so large that DK authorities could not afford to buy their return.

denied access to civilians and prisoners.[27] Thai authorities also allow the assignment of civilians — who may be subject to coercion — to carry supplies across the heavily mined Cambodian border into a war zone.

During a meeting with Foreign Minister Siddhi Savetsila and other Thai officials in January 1987, the Lawyers Committee raised its concerns regarding civilians who wished to leave Site Eight. The Minister said, in essence, that Thailand did not wish to create dissension within the coalition of guerrilla groups by facilitating the movement of civilians from one group to another.[28] He also implied that involuntarily residence at Site Eight is not a serious problem, since the Khmer Rouge "had changed," if only as a practical necessity so that they could continue to attract new recruits.

With respect to the Foreign Minister's principal point, we note that Thailand is able to exert considerable influence over the Khmer Rouge's policies toward the civilians in Site Eight,[29] and urge the Thai government to reconsider its own policy toward those civilians who wish to leave that camp.

---

27. Also, as previously noted, because of Phnom Dey's military nature and because Thai authorities insisted on 24- to 48-hour notice in advance of any deliveries, UNBRO stopped supplying food to the camp in mid-1985.

28. The Deputy Security General of Thailand's National Security Council, Khachadpai Burusapatana, initially replied by asserting that there are also civilians who would wish to leave some of the non-communist camps. When he was reminded that the Khmer Rouge's uniquely appalling human rights record set it apart from other groups, he replied that it should be left to the Khmer Rouge administration to decide whether individuals should be allowed to leave Site Eight. The Committee replied that the whole issue was whether persons involuntarily under Khmer Rouge control should be allowed to leave, and that this problem could not be solved by leaving it to the Khmer Rouge administration.

29. That influence stems not only from the fact that Site Eight is located in Thailand, but also from the broader support that Thailand provides to the guerillas, opposing the PRK.

2. Banishment of Cambodians to Site Eight

One area in which Thai policy has shown marked improvement in the past year involves a former practice by some Thai rangers of banishing Cambodians apprehended in the vicinity of Khao I Dang — typically persons seeking to enter or trade at the camp — to Site Eight for punishment. Between April and the end of December 1985, at least 209 persons were punished in this fashion. Twenty-six of these were registered residents of Khao I Dang.

There was some evidence that Thai rangers carried out personal vendettas against some residents of Khao I Dang by falsely accusing them of trading, thus triggering their relocation to Site Eight. One woman claimed that this had happened to her after she refused a ranger's sexual advances.

To its credit, the Thai government has put a stop to this perverse practice. It appears that no new transfers have taken place since 1985, and all but one of the persons previously transferred have been returned to their prior residences.

VI. PROXIMITY TO THE BORDER

Beyond the daily threats to Cambodians in Thailand posed by fellow Cambodians or Thai security personnel, there looms the potential threat posed by the thousands of Vietnamese and PRK troops stationed along Cambodia's border with Thailand. It was, of course, the Vietnamese army's devastating attacks during the 1984-85 dry season that destroyed the border population's settlements just inside Cambodia, forcing them to flee into Thailand. Though now on Thai territory, the current camps all lie within approximately six miles of the border. The largest concentration, Site Two, lies just over one mile from Cambodia. Only a plain presenting no natural obstacle to attack separates Site Two's 141,000 residents, mostly women and children, from the Vietnamese and People's Republic of Kampuchea (PRK) armies.

The threat is hardly hypothetical. On January 26, 1987, following a skirmish between KPNLF and Vietnamese troops, the Vietnamese army fired three to five retaliatory shells which landed in Dong Ruk, a civilian encampment in Site Two North. According to initial reports, eight or nine civilians were seriously injured.

Though a predicted major Vietnamese offensive during the 1985-86 dry season[1] did not materialize, the constantly shifting military, political and strategic considerations that infuse the Cambodian conflict can give rise to such an offensive or more selective strikes at any time. The border population remains vulnerable.

---

1. See the *Bangkok Voice of Free Asia* in Thai (January 28, 1986) (as reported by FBIS), in which then National Security Council Secretary General Prasong Soonsiri predicted that "Vietnam will attack the refugee camps"; see also the *Bangkok Post* (December 1, 1985), in which Major General Cherdchai Thirathamond forecast that "Vietnam is almost certain to attack the 'Site Two' camp . . . ."

A. Direct Attack or Spillover Fighting

The risk of direct attack against most civilian camps by Vietnamese forces has been diminished by Thailand's policy of separating civilian and military elements of the Cambodian border population. That policy, implemented by the international relief organizations that operate on the border, has brought about a significant improvement over the situation that prevailed when the CGDK forces were located on the Cambodian side of the border. Then, military bases were often located right next to civilian residential areas, and in some areas there was virtually a complete intermingling of military and civilian elements.

The border camps nonetheless remain precariously close to the conflictive frontier zone, exposing the civilian residents to the risk of spillover fighting at the very least, and even direct attack. Some observers believe that the aforementioned shelling of Site Two's Dong Ruk camp on January 26, 1987 was deliberately directed by Vietnamese troops at the civilian encampment. And, as noted below, the continuing threat of direct attack is particularly great with respect to the relatively isolated DK camps in the northern and southern sectors of the border, where separation of military and civilian elements reportedly has not been as effective as at the largest DK camp in Thailand, Site Eight.

The risk of spillover fighting remains high for all of the border camps holding displaced Cambodians. All of them are within range of Vietnamese artillery, as the frequent sound of shelling along the border serves to remind the camp residents. As recently as January 12, 1987, Vietnamese artillery and mortar shells landed near Site Eight. Though the shelling occurred during fighting on the Cambodian side of the border, one shell reportedly damaged one of Site Eight's fences, causing panic among the camp's 30,000 residents, while others landed nearby.[2]

KPNLF troops patrol within a few miles of Site Two, and artillery directed at those troops has at times struck in or near the

---

2. *Bangkok Post* (January 13, 1987).

civilian camps. In March 1986, there was shelling and skirmishing within about six miles of Site Two. In early January 1987, Vietnamese fire reportedly downed a Thai army plane within one or two kilometers of Site Two.[3]

Artillery attacks on Cambodian guerrilla forces have come close enough to Khmer Rouge-controlled Site Eight to force the precautionary evacuation of foreign relief workers at least four times since August 1985. One such barrage in September 1985 prompted the Thai military to return artillery fire and suspend local bus service,[4] while UNBRO ordered the relief workers out of the camp. In early 1985 Thai authorities ordered relief workers out of Site One, then the evacuation site for the Amphil (Ban Sangae) camp, in anticipation of possible shelling by Vietnamese units that had penetrated the border. The Cambodians remained in place, terrified. Fortunately, in this instance there was no exchange of fire.

The southern border area bore the brunt of the fire in the second half of 1986, particularly the DK's Bo Rai and Ta Luan camps. An artillery attack on the latter in early September 1986 left at least eight women and children injured, some of them seriously. The June 11, 1986 Vietnamese shelling of the Thai Red Cross's Kao Larn camp for 200 Cambodian orphans and unaccompanied young adults forced the evacuation of that facility.[5]

The continuing danger of proximity to the border was fatally hammered home on May 29, 1986, when artillery shells landed in the middle of Site Eight, leaving at least 11 dead, including two children, and wounding between 30 and 50 other camp residents, most of whom also were children.[6] Though Thai officials blamed the Vietnamese for the barrage, other observers suspected that the Khmer Rouge were in fact responsible for the shelling.[7] Whatever

---

3. *The Nation* (Bangkok) (January 3, 1987).

4. *Bangkok Post* (September 14, 1985).

5. The camp population subsequently was relocated much further to the north and away from the border.

6. See *Refugee Reports*, Vol. VII, No. 6 (June 13, 1986) at 7.

7. For discussion of this attack, see Chapter V, *supra*.

the source of the attack, the deaths highlighted the vulnerability of the border camps.

Vietnamese offensives against Cambodian guerrillas have often entailed incursions into Thailand, sometimes provoking crossfire that claims civilian casualties. Thai army figures for the period from November 12, 1986 to January 2, 1987 allege 15 incidents of shelling or incursions into Thai soil[8] by the People's Army of Viet Nam (PAVN).

While the likelihood of direct attack against civilian encampments has diminished since mid-1985, when separation of military and civilian elements was substantially achieved, the prospect of spillover fighting remains substantial. Vietnamese troops fortified the border throughout 1985, building roads and moving heavy military equipment along it. In December 1985, Vietnamese tanks were seen poised across the border from FUNCINPEC's Site B, as well as the former KPNLF camp of Dong Ruk, less than three miles from Site Two. Because of similar troop and tank reinforcements just across the border from the KPNLF's O'Bok camp, Thailand and UNBRO evacuated the civilians in early January 1986.[9] More recently, the threat of Vietnamese strikes forced the evacuation of the Khmer Rouge Ta Luan settlement in early April 1986; subsequent artillery attacks were directed against the camp's new location.

In early 1986 at least 2,000 Vietnamese troops were within a few miles of Site Two; previous press estimates were as high as

---

8. At times, Vietnamese troops have taken and held hills located on Thai territory for a number of days. Between 50 and 100 Thai troops were killed repulsing or dislodging Vietnamese forces in 1985 alone. The Thai Foreign Ministry accused the Vietnamese army of seven border violations between September 16 and October 6, 1986, including the seizure of a remote Thai hill for three weeks before being dislodged at the cost of two Thai soldiers' lives. Rodney Tasker, "Dry-season Dominance," *Far Eastern Economic Review* (November 6, 1986) at 42. The Thai military reported utilizing aircraft and heavy weaponry to repulse the Vietnamese force, and claimed that 96 Vietnamese soldiers were killed. *Bangkok Voice of Free Asia* in Thai (October 22, 1986)(as reported by FBIS).

9. *Washington Times* (January 6, 1986).

8,000. In early 1986 there were tens of thousands of Vietnamese along the border or close enough to be dispatched there fairly quickly. Many of these troops were temporarily withdrawn from the border area to battle guerrillas operating deep inside Cambodia. But thousands remained within a day's reach of Site Two, and a gradual build-up along the border reportedly began in October 1986.[10]

The possibility of an attack that could affect the civilian population on the border is greatest during the dry season, the period of little or no rain which lasts from October to May. Because conditions then facilitate the movement of troops and heavy equipment, in recent years — with the exception of 1985/86 — the dry seasons have seen large-scale Vietnamese attacks on military units of the Cambodian guerrilla forces based in or near the civilian camps. Even in the absence of another major offensive during the current 1986/87 dry season, the possibility of selective attacks in the border region heightens during the dry season.[11]

In the event of a direct attack or spillover fighting in the civilian camps, the casualties could be immense. On June 23, 1980, a Vietnamese incursion into Thailand sparked two days of shooting and artillery exchanges. By one estimate, 400 civilians died and 900 were wounded as a result of being caught in the crossfire;[12] most of the casualties were caused by Thai artillery. The Khao I Dang hospital, which takes in only the most serious border casualties, received dozens of civilians in the wake of the January 31, 1983 Vietnamese assault on the KPNLF's Nong Chan camp.

---

10. Thailand's Supreme Command Information Office reported that in October 1986 the Vietnamese and PRK armies reinforced their units in the areas opposite O'Bok pass in Buriram Province with large numbers of additional troops, tanks, armored personnel carriers and artillery. *Bangkok Voice of Free Asia* in Thai (October 21, 1986) (as reported by FBIS). Similar deployments of Vietnamese troops and military equipment have taken place near Site Eight, the KPNLF's Rithisen military camp and Thailand's Surin Province.

11. Even if the potential danger of a major offensive is not realized this year, it will remain hovering just across the border. In this regard, it is worth recalling that the PAVN held back several years before sweeping the entire border population into Thailand and sealing the border in 1984/85.

12. William Shawcross, *The Quality of Mercy* (1984) at 317.

Two artillery attacks on the KPNLF's Sok Sann camp each claimed an undetermined number of lives during the 1984-85 dry season, as did the bombardment of FUNCINPEC's O'Smach camp in 1983. In view of the chaos that erupts when camps are attacked, it is likely that many deaths have gone unreported.

According to a number of sources, the PAVN massacred anywhere from 150 to well over 500 Cambodians when it captured the Khmer Rouge's isolated Paet Um camp on January 5, 1985. Apparently, the Vietnamese surrounded and sealed off the camp before some of the civilians and Khmer Rouge soldiers could escape, and slaughtered those they had trapped. The precise breakdown between civilian and military casualties is not certain, but noncombatants — including unarmed wounded soldiers convalescing at Paet Um's hospital — constituted a sizable portion of the dead.

The Paet Um massacre highlights the risk of future Vietnamese attacks against the four smaller DK camps located along the border's northern and southern sectors. UNBRO believes that some of those civilian encampments "may still be subject to infiltration by non-civilian elements."[13] The presence of military elements in those largely civilian camps could provoke a Vietnamese attack that, while directed against the DK soldiers, would inevitably imperil the civilian population as well.

As indicated above, retaliatory artillery fire by Thai units also could endanger the border population. In the past year there have been artillery exchanges near Site Eight — including several in August 1986 — and other camps. Site Two could be caught in the middle of similar crossfire.

While evacuation sites lie ready in the event of an attack, even they typically are located within the range of Vietnamese artillery fire, sometimes necessitating further relocations. During and after the last Vietnamese offensive, the residents of Sok Sann camp were

13. United Nations Border Relief Operation, *Situation Report as at 9 June 1986* at 1.

relocated four times. Two of the relocations were due to actual shelling, a third from intelligence reports that such an attack was imminent, and the fourth also due to military considerations. The camp remains within striking distance of Vietnamese artillery.

Similarly, Site Three, the planned evacuation area for Site Two, is within reach of Vietnamese firepower. It lies six miles inside Thailand, well within the 17-mile range of the 130mm guns the Vietnamese have placed near the former KPNLF camp of Amphil, inside Cambodia. Even smaller artillery pieces conceivably could hit Site Three, or at least disrupt access to it.

One group of civilians is particularly vulnerable to shelling directed at military targets. These are the civilians living in the "hidden border," made up of logistics/military camps in which CGDK soldiers live with their families and other civilians. The hidden border consists largely, but not exclusively, of Khmer Rouge bases. Because international agencies do not have access to these bases, their civilian population is not known and is not included in UNBRO statistics. But it seems that at least 10,000 civilians, and quite possibly many more, live along the hidden border. Unlike the civilians living in most or all of the United Nations-assisted camps, those who live on the hidden border live among guerrillas.[14]

The threat to the civilian population of the hidden border was underlined on November 5, 1986, when Vietnamese shelling of the KPNLF's Rithisen military camp injured several female relatives of troops based there. One individual died in the attack, though it is not clear whether the victim was a civilian or a soldier.

Finally, life on the precipice takes its toll in ways that reach beyond the Cambodians' physical security. There is the psychological price of knowing an evacuation is just an artillery shell away. Even the semblance of normalcy lies beyond the grasp of lives

---

14. As noted above, UNBRO believes that "some of the smaller northern and southern [civilian] border encampments may still be subject to infiltration by non-civilian elements." United Nations Border Relief Operation, *Situation Report as at 9 June 1986* at 1.

imbued with so much insecurity. And setting up educational systems that will offer the burgeoning population of children some prospects for a productive future, wherever they end up, will remain problematic as long as survival and relocation remain more immediate concerns.

B. Evacuation Risks

In the event of an attack requiring evacuation of civilian camps, a range of security threats could accompany the process. One possibility is that the PAVN could mine the escape routes surrounding the camps, as it did near the KPNLF's Nam Yun camp in December 1984. At least seven civilians died after stepping on mines while fleeing the Vietnamese assault. Several others, including the camp's Cambodian civilian administrator, lost limbs. Even if the Vietnamese army did not plant any mines with a view toward injuring civilians fleeing the camps, there is some risk posed by mines already in place. Thai authorities have, on several occasions in the past year, claimed to have found mines planted by Vietnamese troops a mile or so inside Thailand.[15]

In the event of an attack directed at a Cambodian camp, there is no guarantee that the situation would permit timely evacuation, official assurances notwithstanding. In January 1985, Vietnamese shelling of the Dong Ruk camp's periphery warned of an imminent attack on the large concentration of KPNLF troops there. Thai authorities blocked evacuation of Dong Ruk until shells hit the camp itself, killing 18 civilians, mostly women and children, in what probably has been the greatest loss of civilian lives in the border camps caused solely by artillery fire. In a similar shelling incident in early February 1983, Thai military units stopped 50,000 Cambodians from crossing a tank ditch just inside Thailand and only two miles from the Nong Chan camp, which the Vietnamese had just destroyed. UNBRO appeals to let the Cambodians cross

---

15. *Bangkok Matichon* in Thai (October 27, 1985)(as reported by JPRS); *Bangkok Post* (December 2, 1985 and December 13, 1985).

the ditch and get further away from the Vietnamese went unheeded until PAVN shells started hitting the area. One blast alone claimed seven lives.

Nor is Thai policy the only potential obstacle to evacuation. In November 1984 Chea Chhut, then the KPNLF military commander of the reconstructed Nong Chan camp, delayed for a day a move from the initial evacuation area (Site Three) to a safer location (Site Six), despite Thai permission to proceed. Whatever his rationale — whether he believed his troops could hold off the Vietnamese, or because he feared that an evacuation would place the Nong Chan population under the control of rival KPNLF military commanders and camp administrators — as a result of the delay a shell killed at least one civilian and injured eight others. Similarly, even after the aforementioned shelling of Ta Luan in September 1986 wounded eight of its residents, the Khmer Rouge vetoed UNBRO's request to evacuate the settlement.

The brooding possibility of developments that may require evacuation has at times thwarted other efforts that might enhance the camp residents' general security. When Site Two was established, Task Force 80 considered constructing an elaborate series of fences and ditches around the area. This would have reduced the ability of Thai rangers to wander inside Site Two, where they often abuse the residents.[16] At the same time, it would have prevented Cambodians from straying outside the camp, where they are particularly exposed to brutal punishment by the rangers and regular army cavalry troops.[17] And it would would have also deterred Cambodian bandits seeking to penetrate Site Two.[18] The proposal was ultimately vetoed because the fences and ditches would hamper a smooth evacuation, and could turn out to be a costly investment in a settlement that might later be abandoned. As a result, only a few strands of barbed wire strung around Site Two's perimeter separate the residents of the settlement (and of most other border camps) from those who would do them harm.

---

16. See Chapter III, *supra*.

17. See *id*.

18. See Chapter IV, *supra*.

In the event of an evacuation due to military attack, shelling could disrupt the supply of water, medicine and food to an evacuated population. Given Site Two's population of 141,000 — by far the largest concentration of Cambodians along the border since 1980 — its Cambodian residents are seriously threatened by such disruption. It would take a full day, free of interruption by shelling or fighting, to supply water to Site Three, the evacuation area for Site Two. Thai officials acknowledge that a shortage of clean water could rapidly spawn epidemics of fatal diseases, such as severe infant diarrhea.

The nature of the camp population further complicates the evacuation process. According to statistics compiled by UNBRO, 25 percent of the inhabitants are less than five years old.[19] As many as 2,000 of the border camp residents have artificial legs, victims of the mine-strewn border area.[20] UNBRO and the ICRC endeavor to transport women in the late stages of pregnancy, as well as seriously ill and wounded patients, in advance of a general evacuation, circumstances permitting.

Again, Site Two poses the greatest problems, by virtue of its size and vulnerability. Between 800 and 1,000 residents would require the initial UNBRO/ICRC evacuation, not counting the family members who sometimes accompany such cases. At least 100 patients needing oxygen equipment would be moved to Khao I Dang. These figures exclude those civilians who might be injured by shelling or fighting, who also would be taken to the nearest major medical facility, located in Khao I Dang. Even if unimpeded by traffic or military activity, driving on the rough roads linking Site Two to Khao I Dang during the daytime takes an hour. At night, with shells and panic in the air, the ride would be longer and more perilous.

Absent such developments, the combined experience of UNBRO, the ICRC, Thai authorities and the Cambodian camp

---

19. The border camps may have the highest birth rate in the world: reportedly 40 births a day, or a growth rate of five percent. *Bangkok Post* (August 25, 1985).

20. *Reuters* dispatch (January 3, 1985); See also "Vietnam thinks again," *The Economist* (May 24, 1986) at 44.

administrations could contribute to smooth evacuations in the event of an attack. But the serious impediments to a smooth evacuation are many.

C. Recommendations

Though nations hosting persons displaced by a neighboring country's upheavals generally are free to determine where those persons can temporarily settle, humanitarian considerations may warrant care on the part of the host country to locate them a safe distance away from armed hostilities. It is for this reason that the UNHCR generally seeks to locate refugees at least 30 miles away from the border, particularly in conflictive situations.

In contrast, none of the Cambodian settlements in Thailand is farther than six miles from the border. The recent history of incursions onto Thai soil by Vietnamese armed forces underscores the very real threat posed by the proximity of the Cambodian settlements in Thailand to the conflictive border.

Nevertheless, Thailand has thus far declined to follow the recommendation of UNBRO, some representatives of the U.S. government, and others that the residents of Site Two be moved to its evacuation site, located approximately six miles from the border. Instead, the Thai government has indicated that it will follow its past practice of precautionary evacuations in advance of actual attacks.[21]

But, as past experience has proven, such evacuations implemented, literally, "under the gun" have all too often been perilous, and too many innocent lives have been lost in their execution. Accordingly, the Lawyers Committee believes that the security of the Cambodians on the border would be greatly enhanced if their settlements were moved further away from the border.

---

21. See United States Department of State, *Report of the Indochinese Refugee Panel* (April 1986) at 29.

93

VII. THE CLOSING OF KHAO I DANG

On December 29, 1986, Thailand announced that the Khao I Dang holding center, home to some 24,000 Cambodians, would be closed two days later. Prasong Soonsiri, Secretary General of the Office of the Prime Minister, declared that the camp's residents would be transferred to the border in a phased removal program.[1]

The announcement climaxed what had become an impassioned public debate over the fate of Khao I Dang, touched off by Thailand's announcement in June 1986 that Khao I Dang and its Annex would be closed by year-end and that those residents not accepted for third-country resettlement would be moved closer to the border.[2] The announcement provoked strong opposition by concerned organizations and some governments; their reaction is some measure of Khao I Dang's power as a symbol. Since its establishment in 1979, Khao I Dang has been a transit point for many of the 200,000 Cambodians accepted for resettlement in other countries. For others, it has provided a place of temporary asylum, where those who do not wish to align themselves with any of the guerrilla factions who administer the border settlements could nonetheless find shelter following their flight from Cambodia. In the words of one correspondent, Khao I Dang has become "a symbol of hope to hundreds of thousands of Cambodians escaping a decade of death and dislocation."[3]

Beyond the symbolism, Khao I Dang in fact provides better security to its residents than do the border settlements, for two reasons in particular. First, residents of Khao I Dang — unlike the border population — receive assistance from the United Nations High Commissioner for Refugees (UNHCR). The Geneva-based organization has an explicit protection mandate,[4] as well as

---

1. See Barbara Crossette, "Thai Refugee Camp, Door of Hope, Will Be Closed," *The New York Times* (December 30, 1986).
2. See *The Nation* (Bangkok) (June 19, 1986).
3. Barbara Crossette, "Thai Refugee Camp, Door of Hope, Will Be Closed," *The New York Times* (December 30, 1986).
4. Statute of the Office of the United Nations High Commissioner for Refugees, Ch. 1.

considerable experience in troubled regions throughout the world in implementing that mandate. Second, located farther away from the conflictive Thai-Cambodian border than any other camp for Cambodians in Thailand, Khao I Dang has offered its residents greater security from the perils that affect the border population.[5]

Although Khao I Dang itself has been closed, these protections need not be lost. The Lawyers Committee strongly urges the Thai government, as it moves to implement its decision to close Khao I Dang, to preserve the camp residents' status as asylum-seekers subject to the jurisdiction of the UNHCR.[6] Additionally, we urge the government to ensure that none of Khao I Dang's residents are moved to a location that is less secure than their current site.

A. Thai Policy Regarding the Future of Khao I Dang's Residents

Thailand's decision to close Khao I Dang reflects two primary and interrelated concerns. First, the decision stands as a rebuke to third countries whose acceptance of Cambodians for resettlement has fallen off sharply in recent years. "The West could have done more than this," Squadron Leader Prasong told a correspondent after his formal announcement in late December that Khao I Dang would be closed. "But so many have only promised, and have taken no action," he said.[7] Indeed, anticipating the closing of Khao I Dang earlier in 1986, the Thai government asked resettlement nations to complete their processing of the remaining population at Khao I Dang[8] and, according to Prasong, delayed closing the camp

---

5. For discussion of the security threats affecting that population, see Chapter VI, *supra.*

6. As elaborated in Chapter VIII, the Lawyers Committee also recommends that UNHCR's protection mandate be extended to include the displaced Cambodians on the border as well.

7. Barbara Crossette, "Thai Refugee Camp, Door of Hope, Will Be Closed," *The New York Times* (December 30, 1986).

8. See United States Department of State, *Progress Report: Recommendations of the Indochinese Refugee Panel* (September 1986) at 15.

at the request of Western governments only to see no significant increase in their rate of acceptance of camp residents.[9]

Second, the decision reflects Thailand's belief that, despite the fact that it has not allowed Cambodians who entered Khao I Dang after August 1984 to be processed for third-country resettlement (see below), the camp continues to serve as a magnet for Cambodians who hope to emigrate despite Thai policy.[10]

At a press conference on December 29, 1986, Squadron Leader Prasong described a phased-removal process of implementing the decision to close Khao I Dang. First to be moved will be some 7,000 ration card-holders (RC's), who arrived at Khao I Dang after August 1984 and lived there surreptitiously without documentation until Task Force 80 authorized their registration for food distribution on September 29, 1985. Having used the registration to bring the RC's out of the underground existence they had been leading, Task Force 80 then moved them to the newly-constructed Khao I Dang Annex in December 1985. This group is to be given the choice of moving to Site B or to the KPNLF's Site Two.[11]

The next group to be moved are some 3,000 residents who entered Khao I Dang between February 1983 and August 1984. Though this group entered illegally, the Thai government regularized their status in August 1984, granting them "family cards." The family card-holders (FC's) were entitled to remain in Khao I Dang and receive food rations, and the Thai government eventually granted the United States and other nations permission to begin considering the FC's for refugee resettlement. The group that has not been accepted for resettlement is to be moved to FUNCINPEC's Site B.[12]

9. Barbara Crossette, "Thai Refugee Camp, Door of Hope, Will Be Closed," *The New York Times* (December 30, 1986).

10. Press Release from Prime Minister's Office announcing closing of Khao I Dang (December 29, 1986).

11. See *id.*

12. See Barbara Crossette, "Thai Refugee Camp, Door of Hope, Will Be Closed," *The New York Times* (December 30, 1986).

Finally, a group of 14,000 residents who entered Khao I Dang before February 1983 — previously the cut-off date for eligibility for third-country resettlement processing — will be moved to "a suitable site along the border as they prefer."[13] Most of the Cambodians in this group have been rejected for resettlement in the United States, some pursuant to a controversial screening program designed to exclude persons responsible for Khmer Rouge atrocities during the late 1970s.[14]

Significantly, Thailand's Foreign Minister indicated that residents of Khao I Dang who can now be considered for resettlement in third countries will not lose this status even after they are removed to other sites.[15] Of even greater relevance to the

---

13. Press Release of the Office of the Foreign Minister announcing closing of Khao I Dang (December 29, 1986).

14. Various studies have concluded, either implicitly or explicitly, that the applications of many of these Cambodians were evaluated by unfair procedures. In essence, those studies concluded that many of the rejected applicants were arbitrarily identified as persecutors because of supposed involvement in Khmer Rouge atrocities, and were excluded on this basis. See, e.g., Staff of Senate Committee on Foreign Relations, S. Rpt. 240, 98th Cong., 2d Sess., U.S. Processing of Khmer Refugees (1984); see also David Hawk, *Khmer Rouge Screening and Cambodian Refugees in Thailand* (May 15, 1984), Appendix II to Staff of Senate Committee on Foreign Relations; Stephen Heder, *The Case of Nop Tha: An Evaluation of the Evidence as Presented* (May 3, 1984), Attachment B to Hawk; Stephen Golub, *Looking for Phantoms: Flaws in the Khmer Rouge Screening Process*, a United States Committee for Refugees Issue Brief (April 1986); John Jensen, submission to Rep. Daniel Lungren (February 20, 1985); Letter from UNHCR Representative in Thailand Jaques Terlin to INS District Director John Schroeder (July 9, 1984); James E. Mitchell, Report on Impressions Following a Week in Bangkok, Thailand, April 13-21, 1985, Reviewing Khmer Refugee Policy and Practice (1985) (unpublished manuscript); Hanna Sophie Greve, Double, Double, Toil and Trouble — Khmer Rouge Captives Face Continued Injustice (September 1984) (unpublished manuscript).

While The Lawyers Committee has not conducted its own study of the so-called "Khmer Rouge screening process," we believe that the review process should be reopened. In this regard we note that, in response to criticism of that process, the Immigration and Nationalization Service undertook limited reviews of the rejected population. These have only been afforded to a relatively low percentage of the rejected population, and have resulted in only a small portion of those reviewed being accepted for resettlement.

15. Meeting between Floyd Abrams, Diane Orentlicher and Foreign Minister Siddhi Savetsila (January 7, 1987).

Committee's protection-related concerns, Thailand appears willing to consider allowing the UNHCR to continue to provide protection to the Khao I Dang residents, wherever they are relocated.[16]

B. Recommendations

Wherever the residents of Khao I Dang are moved, the Lawyers Committee regards it of utmost importance that they not lose their special status as a result of that move. In particular, they should continue to be able to avail themselves of UNHCR's protection.

Additionally, the Lawyers Committee believes that the Khao I Dang population should be provided the opportunity to move to a safe, neutral location. We do not believe that the options announced by the Thai government in late December adequately serve this objective. As detailed in Chapter VI, Cambodians now living in the settlements to which the Khao I Dang population is to be moved face the brooding threat of attack by hostile armed forces entrenched on the other side of the border; one of those camps, Site Two, was shelled as recently as January 26, 1987. Removing the Khao I Dang population to those settlements would simply enlarge the numbers endangered by that threat.

Additionally, removal of Khao I Dang's residents to existing border settlements may expose them to a hostile population. Those in Khao I Dang are perceived by many Cambodians on the border as having "voted with their feet" not to support the guerrilla groupings to which the border settlements are linked. Accordingly, we urge the Thai government to consider establishing a separate site —

---

16. The press release announcing the closing of Khao I Dang seemed to leave open the possibility of such a future role for UNHCR: "The protection of Kampucheans removed to the border area will be under [the] responsibility of an international organization considered appropriate by the Secretary General of the United Nations and the coordination between UNBRO and UNHCR." Additionally, in a meeting with the Lawyers Committee on January 7, 1987, Prime Minister Siddhi expressed some measure of receptivity to the possibility of UNHCR continuing to have jurisdiction over the current population at Khao I Dang wherever they are relocated.

a safe distance away from the border — to which Khao I Dang's residents can elect to be transferred.

Consistent with their continued status as UNHCR-assisted asylum-seekers, the Khao I Dang population should also continue to be protected against involuntary repatriation. At the same time, we believe that the impending transition presents an opportune time to re-invigorate the long-protracted and singularly unsuccessful negotiations between the Thai government and the PRK to establish a program of voluntary repatriation. Finally, the Committee welcomes the previously-noted indications by the Thai government that it will continue to allow the Khao I Dang population to be considered for third-country resettlement opportunities after they are moved.

VIII. LEGAL PROTECTION, HUMANITARIAN PRINCIPLES AND THE ROLE OF HUMANITARIAN ORGANIZATIONS

A. Legal Protection and Humanitarian Principles

An island of relative stability in a frequently volatile region, Thailand has hosted hundreds of thousands who have taken flight from the turmoil engulfing her war-torn neighbors. Despite its long history of sheltering such people, Thailand has generally avoided assuming legally binding obligations toward them. Most notably, it has signed neither the 1951 Convention Relating to the Status of Refugees nor its 1967 Protocol, and does not recognize the Cambodians who are the subject of this report as "refugees." Under Thai law, Cambodians and other Indochinese in Thai camps are "displaced persons."[1] By virtue of having violated the pertinent Thai statutes upon entering the country, they are considered "illegal entrants" or "illegal immigrants."[2]

Nevertheless, Thailand has allowed the United Nations High Commissioner for Refugees (UNHCR) to assist "displaced persons" in Khao I Dang and its Annex,[3] and has implicitly permitted the organization a protection role with respect to the residents of those camps.[4] Thailand also professes to act "in accordance with

---

1. Clause 3 of "Regulations concerning displaced persons from neighboring countries," issued by the Royal Thai Government Ministry of Interior on April 8, 1954, as cited in Muntarbhorn, *Displaced Persons in Thailand: Legal and National Policy Issues in Perspective*, 1 Chulalongkorn Law Review 5, 8 (1982).

2. Article 58 of the Royal Thai Government's 1979 Immigration Act, as cited in Muntarbhorn, *supra*, at 11.

3. Agreements between UNHCR and Thailand, dated July 30, 1975 and December 22, 1975, as cited in Muntarbhorn, *Protection and Assistance of Refugees in Armed Conflicts and Internal Disturbances: A Re-Appraisal of the Institutional Competence of the Red Cross and the Office of the United Nations High Commissioner for Refugees*, 2 Chulalongkorn Law Review 1, 3 n.3 (1983).

4. *Id.* at 3 n.3.

humanitarian principles together with the consideration of our sovereignty, national security and interests."[5]

Evolving interpretations of such "humanitarian principles" suggest that, despite their lack of refugee status in Thailand, the Cambodians there should be assured physical protection. According to the UNHCR, there is "an increasing recognition" that persons, who, like many of the Cambodians in Thailand, have fled their homelands due to armed conflict merit protection and at least temporary asylum.[6]

Moreover, providing such persons with direct physical protection "remains the primary responsibility of the countries where the refugees find themselves" — in this case Thailand.[7] In particular, armed attacks around the globe "clearly demonstrate the importance for refugees to be settled away from the border area. . . ."[8]

The United Nations General Assembly has reaffirmed the application of humanitarian principles in a general way by condemning "all violations of the rights and safety of refugees and asylum-seekers,"[9] including armed attacks and other forms of brutality, and by urging all states "to take all measures necessary to ensure the safety of refugees and asylum-seekers."[10]

To be sure, humanitarian principles govern the behavior of Vietnamese and PRK troops as well. PAVN attacks on civilian

---

5. Transcript of address by Squadron Leader Prasong Soonsiri, at 1985 Committee for the Coordination of Services to Displaced Persons in Thailand Annual Conference on Indochinese Displaced Persons in Thailand (July 18, 1985) at 6.

6. Report of the U.N. High Commissioner for Refugees, 40 U.N. GAOR Supp. (No. 12) at 4-5, U.N. Doc. A/40/12 (1985).

7. Report of the U.N. High Commissioner for Refugees, 38 U.N. GAOR Supp. (No. 12) at 8, U.N. Doc. A/38/12 (1983).

8. Report of the U.N. High Commissioner for Refugees, 36 U.N. GAOR Supp. (No. 12) at 8, U.N. Doc. A/36/12 (1981).

9. G.A. Res. 140, 39 U.N. GAOR Supp. (No. 51) at 228, U.N. Doc. A/39/140 (1984).

10. *Id.*

settlements affiliated with the CGDK guerrillas have at times violated the Geneva Convention Relative to the Protection of Civilian Persons in Time of War and its Protocol I,[11] and have flown in the face of several General Assembly resolutions.[12]

B. The Role of Humanitarian Organization

Humanitarian principles recognizing the protection-related rights of displaced persons are only as effective as the institutions that safeguard those rights. Despite the substantial security threats faced by the border camp residents, none of the international organizations providing assistance to them plays a comprehensive protection role. UNBRO, which provides humanitarian assistance to all of the border camps as well as to some 80,000 "affected Thai villagers," has no explicit protection mandate, though it plays an important supportive role with respect to the ICRC's role as "lead agency" with respect to protection matters affecting the border population (see below). While the UNHCR has a protection mandate in Khao I Dang and its Annex, that mandate extends to only ten percent of the 270,000 Cambodians living in civilian camps in Thailand. As noted in Chapter VII, it has not yet been determined whether UNHCR will continue to have jurisdiction over even that population once Thailand implements its decision to close Khao I Dang and its Annex. And while the ICRC has a protection mandate with respect to the border population, its protection role has been limited, in part because of limited staff resources, limitations on its own interpretation of its protection role, and, until last year, inadequate coordination with other concerned agencies.[13]

---

11. See Geneva Conventions of August 12, 1949, common article 3; see also Protocol I to Geneva Conventions of August 12, 1949, articles 48, 51, 57, and 86. Vietnam became a party to the Geneva Conventions in 1957, and to Protocol I in 1981.

12. See G.A. Res. 195, 37 U.N. GAOR Supp. (No. 51) at 212, U.N. Doc. A/37/195 (1982); see also G.A. Res. 3, 38 U.N. GAOR Supp. (No. 40) at 14, U.N. Doc. A/38/40 (1983); Report of the U.N. High Commissioner for Refugees, 38 U.N. GAOR Supp. (No. 12) at 8-9, U.N. Doc. A/38/12 (1983).

13. The ICRC's protection-related activities on the Thai-Cambodian border have centered on several roles. It is actively involved in the process of evacuating the civilian border population in the event of attack, and generally seeks to ensure that the military and civilian populations are kept separate. It also has been particularly active in providing protection, as well as humanitarian assistance, to the displaced Vietnamese in Thailand.

In November 1985, the U.N. Secretary General's Special Representative for the Coordination of Kampuchean Humanitarian Assistance Programs informed Thailand's Foreign Minister that these three international organizations would coordinate their activities to try to ensure greater security for the Cambodian population on the border, with the ICRC acting as the "lead agency" with respect to protection matters there. Under this arrangement, representations to the Thai government regarding security incidents are presented by the ICRC, while UNBRO compiles much of the information that forms the basis of the ICRC's interventions.

Although the Lawyers Committee welcomed this development, we do not believe the arrangement offers sufficient protection to the Cambodians. While the ICRC has achieved some measure of success in obtaining the release of Cambodians and Vietnamese held for ransom by KPNLF troops when the former are intercepted while en route to Thailand,[14] it has apparently been less effective in curbing abuses committed in Thailand.

The Lawyers Committee believes that the security of the Cambodian border population would be enhanced if one of the major humanitarian organizations operating there assumed a significantly more active and comprehensive protection role. This would address a vital need: a mechanism should be in place for monitoring, reporting, and effectively responding to abuses as they occur, on an ongoing basis.

And, as elaborated in Chapter IV.B., it has helped secure the release of Cambodians and Vietnamese detained on their way to Thailand by KPNLF troops.

Another aspect of the ICRC's protection role on the border has been its efforts to visit prisoners. In late 1984, it obtained access to prisoners held in areas administered by the two non-communist guerrilla parties to the CGDK. Since then, its access to such detention facilities has been restricted. The ICRC does visit Vietnamese "illegal immigrants" detained by Thai authorities at a military prison in Aranyaprathet, but has been denied access to Vietnamese soldiers detained by Thai authorities.

14. See Chapter IV.B., *supra*.

Equally important, the agency that serves that function must receive the full cooperation of the Thai government. For the agency to be effective, the Thai government must recognize that that agency has the right and responsibility to bring security problems to the attention of responsible Thai authorities. The Thai government should also cooperate with the agency by providing it information, if only on a confidential basis, about action taken in response to reported abuses.

While any of the three major international organizations operating in Thailand — the ICRC, UNBRO and the UNHCR — conceivably could serve this function, the UNHCR may be the most appropriate of the three to do so. It has an explicit protection mandate, as well as considerable experience in implementing that mandate in troubled regions throughout the world. And, in our view, any previous justification for limiting the reach of that mandate to exclude the Cambodians on the Thai-Cambodian border no longer has force.

One of the principal justifications for the fact that UNHCR's mandate does not extend to the border population is that, historically, that group lived on the Cambodian side of the border, and the UNHCR's mandate encompasses persons "outside the country of [their] nationality."[15] Since their flight to Thailand two years ago, the Cambodian border population has come within that standard. Thailand's decision to close Khao I Dang[16] presents an opportune moment to re-examine and re-define the UNHCR's role in Thailand. In Chapter VII, we urged that UNHCR's mandate over the Cambodians now living in Khao I Dang be allowed, in effect, to "follow" that population wherever they are resettled. As the Thai government considers the UNHCR's future role with respect to the Cambodians who will be removed from Khao I Dang, we urge it to consider extending the UNHCR's protection mandate to encompass the entire border population of displaced Cambodians.

---

15. UNHCR Statute, paragraph 6B.
16. See Chapter VII, *supra.*

Finally, we believe that the security of the displaced Cambodians would be enhanced if there were an international relief presence in the camps at night, particularly if such personnel were equipped with radios that would enable them to contact Task Force 80 in the event of an attack against camp residents. As we have noted elsewhere,[17] most of the violent attacks against Cambodians have occurred at night, when there typically is no such presence.

---

17. See Chapter IV, *supra*.

APPENDIX A

SYNOPSES OF PRESS ACCOUNTS OF CRIMINAL ACTS BY THAI RANGERS[1]

— "Five people were killed and 20 others injured when an allegedly drunk ranger threw a hand grenade into a crowd at a temple fair . . ."[2]

— Following the arrest of two colleagues for assaulting a policeman, 40 rangers attacked a police station with M-16 rifles and grenade launchers, firing over 100 shots and injuring at least three people before pulling back.[3]

— A ranger shot dead two fellow rangers and seriously wounded two others, mistakenly thinking they were a group that had assaulted him earlier.[4]

— Following the arrest of six drunken comrades, 50 armed rangers surrounded a police station.[5]

— According to at least 20 witnesses, three policemen who disappeared and are presumed dead were last seen being taken away by armed rangers in a pickup truck after being stopped by the rangers at a checkpoint.[6]

— "Two rangers reportedly killed a man and seriously wounded his wife and daughter-in-law . . ."[7]

---

1. The articles cited herein concern ranger violence against Thai victims. There have been few newspaper accounts of ranger abuses against Cambodians, a subject addressed in Chapter III.A., perhaps reflecting pressures on Thai journalists not to report such practices.

2. *Bangkok Post* (January 17,1985).

3. *Bangkok Post* (December 16,1984).

4. *Bangkok Post* (September 9, 1984).

5. *Bangkok Post* (June 23, 1984).

6. *Bangkok Post* (February 18, 1984).

7. *Bangkok Post* (January 25, 1984).

— "Three young rangers are being detained at Don Muang police station after they allegedly admitted on Thursday night to killing a fellow ranger . . ."[8]

— Three rangers tortured and killed a fourth after arguing over property the group had stolen.[9]

— "Eight people were killed and 46 injured when a [drunken] ranger lobbed a hand grenade into a crowd of cinema spectators at a temple fair. . . ."[10]

— "An army-trained ranger was arrested by police and charged with conspiring with another ranger to attack a . . . dance stage with a hand grenade during a fair in mid-December, killing two persons and wounding 41 others."[11]

— "Last week the Army admitted that a group of rangers, trying to flush out communist insurgents, were responsible for a massacre in Nakhon Si Thammarat earlier this year in which 11 people died."[12]

— "A heavily armed band of rangers stormed into Muang District police station on Friday night, shot open a cell lock to free a detained colleague and escaped in a commandeered truck after battling with pursuing police and marines" and killing the truck's driver.[13]

8. *Bangkok Post* (June 18, 1983).
9. *Bangkok Post* (November 4, 1983).
10. *Bangkok Post* (February 22, 1982).
11. *Bangkok Post* (January 1, 1982).
12. *Bangkok Post* (October 28, 1981).
13. *Bangkok Post* (October 25, 1981).

APPENDIX B

GLOSSARY

Chamkar Ko:

KPNLF military base along the Thai-Cambodian border at which Vietnamese and Cambodians fleeing their homelands often have been detained for ransom and sexually abused; affiliated with the Nong Samet civilian camp

Chea Chhut:

KPNLF military commander of the Nong Chan civilian camp and the affiliated Nong Chan military base at least until late November 1986, when the KPNLF claims to have transferred him to a base along the border for retraining and reassignment in the Cambodian interior

CGDK:

Coalition Government of Democratic Kampuchea

Coalition Government of Democratic Kampuchea:

Tripartite coalition of forces opposing the Vietnamese occupation of Cambodia; backed by Thailand, the United States and China, and consisting of the KPNLF, FUNCINPEC and the DK. The CGDK is the government of the state of Democratic Kampuchea, which holds the Cambodia seat at the United Nations

Democratic Kampuchea:

The government of Cambodia from 1975 to 1979, when, under the leadership of Pol Pot, it presided over the deaths of one million or more Cambodians; now a guerrilla force which is a party to the CGDK; commonly known as the "Khmer Rouge"

DK:

Democratic Kampuchea

Dong Ruk:

KPNLF civilian camp which is now part of Site Two North

FUNCINPEC:

French acronym for National United Front for an Independent, Neutral, Peaceful and Cooperative Cambodia

"Hidden border":

String of CGDK military/logistics bases along Thai-Cambodian border, holding approximately 10,000 civilians who are beyond the observation of international organizations; includes Phnom Dey, Rithisen, the Nong Chan military base, and Chamkar Ko

ICRC:

International Committee of the Red Cross

International Committee of the Red Cross:

A Geneva-based humanitarian organization, the ICRC provides protection and assistance to victims of international and civil wars and of internal disturbances and tensions on a neutral basis. Its activities in Thailand include evacuating the border population in the event of attack by Vietnamese forces; seeking to maintain a physical separation between the military and civilian elements of the Cambodian border population; providing humanitarian assistance and protection to the displaced Vietnamese living in Thailand; visiting Vietnamese "illegal immigrants" detained by Thai authorities at a military prison in Aranyaprathet; and running a surgical hospital at Khao I Dang

Khao I Dang:

UNHCR-assisted holding center from which Cambodians have been considered for resettlement in third countries; located further inside Thailand than the Cambodian border camps, and not considered to be one of the border camps. Thailand officially closed Khao I Dang as of December 31, 1986, though its population has not yet been relocated.

Khao I Dang Annex:

UNHCR-assisted camp adjacent to Khao I Dang; holds Cambodians who entered Khao I Dang after August 1984, and whom the Thai government therefore bars from consideration for resettlement in third countries. Like Khao I Dang, the Annex was officially closed at the end of 1986.

Khmer People's National Liberation Front:

A non-communist grouping opposing the Vietnamese occupation of Cambodia; the largest party to the CGDK (in terms of the civilian population of affiliated camps). The KPNLF's President is Son Sann, who was the Cambodian Prime Minister in the 1960's; for over a year, a dissident faction that includes the Front's Commander-in-Chief, Gen. Sak Sutsakhan, has opposed Son Sann.

Khmer Rouge:

The name by which the DK guerrilla group commonly is known

KPNLF:

Khmer People's National Liberation Front

National United Front for an Independent, Neutral, Peaceful and Cooperative Cambodia:

A non-communist grouping opposing the Vietnamese occupation of Cambodia; also known by its French acronym, "FUNCINPEC"; its titular leader is Prince Norodom Sihanouk, who presided over the government of the Kingdom of Cambodia from 1953 until 1970

3

Nong Chan:

Refers to both a KPNLF civilian camp which is now part of Site Two North and to an affiliated military base by the same name, at which Vietnamese and Cambodians fleeing their homelands often have been detained for ransom and abused; both were under the command of Chea Chhut until his reported transfer in late November 1986

Nong Samet:

KPNLF civilian camp which constitutes Site Two South; affiliated with the Chamkar Ko and Rithisen military bases, which were commanded by Liv Ne until his reported transfer in November 1986

(Prince) Norodom Sihanouk:

Presided over the government of the Kingdom of Cambodia from 1953, when he declared the nation's independence from France, until 1970, when his government was deposed in a military coup; now the titular leader of FUNCINPEC

PAVN:

People's Army of Viet Nam

People's Republic of Kampuchea:

Vietnamese-backed government of Cambodia, whose titular head is Heng Samrin

Phnom Dey:

DK military/logistics base holding several thousand civilians; also known as ''Site Eight North''

Pol Pot:

De facto DK military and political leader when the DK ruled Cambodia in the late 1970's, as well as afterwards, when it became a guerrilla force opposing the PRK

PRK:

People's Republic of Kampuchea

Rangers:

Thai paramilitary troops that, among other functions, operate under the command of Task Force 80 officers in guarding Cambodian civilian camps in Thailand

Rithisen:

KPNLF military base along the Thai-Cambodian border, at which Vietnamese and Cambodians fleeing their homelands often have been detained for ransom and abused; commanded by Liv Ne until his reported transfer in late November 1986, and affiliated with the Nong Samet civilian camp

Samrong Kiat:

DK civilian camp located in the northern section of the Thai-Cambodian border area

Site B:

FUNCINPEC's only civilian camp in Thailand, located in the northern section of the Thai-Cambodian border area

Site Eight:

The largest DK civilian camp, located in the central section of the Thai-Cambodian border area

Site Seven:

Former interim location, next to Khao I Dang, for the KPNLF's Nong Samet camp during early to mid-1985; established after a Vietnamese offensive drove the Nong Samet population into Thailand, and existed until that population was moved back to the border, to Site Two South

Site Three:

Planned evacuation area for Site Two in event of a Vietnamese/PRK military attack; also the designation in November 1984 of a different location to which the Nong Chan population temporarily was evacuated

Site Two:

Collection of five civilian KPNLF camps and one small Vietnamese camp; the largest concentration of displaced Cambodians along the Thai-Cambodian border since 1980; situated in the central section of the Thai-Cambodian border area

Site Two North:

Location of four civilian KPNLF camps: Dong Ruk, San Ro, Ban Sangae and Nong Chan

Site Two South:

Location of the civilian KPNLF camp of Nong Samet; though the term "Site Two South" generally refers exclusively to Nong Samet, a small Vietnamese civilian camp also is situated in Site Two South

Sok Sann:

KPNLF civilian camp in the southern section of the Thai-Cambodian border area

Son Sann:

A Prime Minister of Cambodia under Prince Sihanouk during the 1960's; now the President of the KPNLF

Squadron Leader Prasong Soonsiri:

Secretary General of the Office of the Prime Minister of Thailand, and a leading Thai policy-maker regarding displaced Indochinese

Ta Luan:

DK civilian camp in the southern section of the Thai-Cambodian border area

Task Force 838:

A Thai military border unit involved in the transfer to the ICRC of Vietnamese and Cambodian detainees released from the Chamkar Ko, Rithisen and Nong Chan military bases

Task Force 80:

A Thai military unit created in 1980 to supervise and provide security for displaced Cambodians in Thailand and on the Thai-Cambodian border

UNBRO:

United Nations Border Relief Operation

UNHCR:

United Nations High Commissioner for Refugees

United Nations Border Relief Operation

Established in 1982 to provide emergency humanitarian relief assistance to some quarter of a million displaced Cambodians living along the Thai-Cambodian border, as well as to some Thai villagers who have been adversely affected by the recurrent border hostilities and by the presence of the Cambodians at the border; responsible for providing food, shelter, relief materials, health care and sanitation, elementary education and support for social services to the border population; assisted in supplying humanitarian relief by a number of private voluntary agencies

United Nations High Commissioner for Refugees:

A Geneva-based United Nations organ with a mandate to assist and protect refugees and persons in refugee-like situations; has been responsible for providing protection to and co-ordinating

the provision of humanitarian services to the displaced Cambodian populations in Khao I Dang, the Khao I Dang Annex, and
Phanat Nikhom, but is not involved with the much larger
population of displaced Cambodians along the Thai-
Cambodian border

UNBRO-ASSISTED CAMPS (BORDER CAMPS)[1]

Name of Camp	CGDK Affiliation	Approximate Population
Northern Sector		
Samrong Kiat	DK	8,000
Natrao	DK	12,000
Site B	FUNCINPEC	38,000
Central Sector		
Dong Ruk (Site Two North)	KPNLF	18,000
San Ro (Site Two North)	KPNLF	11,000
Ban Sangae (Site Two North)	KPNLF	28,000
Nong Chan (Site Two North)	KPNLF	24,000
Nong Samet (Site Two South)	KPNLF	58,000
Vietnamese (Site Two South)	—	3,000
Site Eight	DK	30,000
Southern Sector		
Bo Rai	DK	3,000
Sok Sann	KPNLF	7,000
Ta Luan	DK	4,000
Total:		246,000[2]

---

1. The figures provided here are derived from United Nations Border Relief Operation, *Situation Report as at August 15, 1986* at 8. Beyond the camp populations listed above, an estimated 10,000 additional civilian Cambodians live in military logistics bases along the Thai-Cambodian border, and receive no U.N. assistance.

2. Because the individual camp population figures are rounded off, adding them up to arrive at totals for CGDK affiliation and geographical sector populations would produce sums slightly lower than some of the totals provided elsewhere in this report or than the total border population figure provided here.

CAMBODIAN POPULATIONS OF UNHCR-ASSISTED CAMPS[1]

Name of Camp	Approximate Population
Khao I Dang and Annex	24,000
Phanat Nikhom[2]	2,000
Kap Cherng[3]	1,000
Total:	27,000

---

1. These figures are derived from U.S. Department of State, Bureau for Refugee Programs, *Indochinese Refugee Activity: Monthly Report for October 1986* at 10.
2. Phanat Nikhom is a transit and processing center holding displaced persons from all Indochinese groups in Thailand, including Cambodians who have been accepted for resettlement abroad and Cambodians who fled their homeland by sea.
3. Kap Cherng holds Cambodian nationals of ethnic Thai origin who are seeking to regularize their status in Thailand through acquisition of Thai citizenship or other means.